"Rarely have I re
me and yet holds out the hand of hope."

Sir Tim Smit, FOUNDER OF THE EDEN PROJECT

THE UNSUSTAINABLE TRUTH

How Investing for the Future is Destroying the Planet and What to Do About It

DR DAVID KO AND RICHARD BUSELLATO

The Unsustainable Truth

First published in 2021 by

Panoma Press Ltd
48 St Vincent Drive, St Albans, Herts, AL1 5SJ, UK
info@panomapress.com
www.panomapress.com

Book layout by Neil Coe.

978-1-784529-59-8

Dedication

To our children, their children, and their children's children...

Testimonials

"Rarely have I read a book that has so troubled me and yet holds out the hand of hope."

Sir Tim Smit, founder of the Eden Project

"For sustainability, governments, businesses and individuals face their choices at best complementary. This book tells vividly how the choices of an individual, on the basis of ethics or economics, impact the outcome."

Erkki Liikanen, former Finance Minister and Central Bank Governor of Finland

Acknowledgements

We start by thanking our families for giving us the inspiration and putting up with us to write this book. They supported us in more ways than merely the initial readings and feedback they offered, providing us with space during the Coronavirus lockdown. They have our deepest gratitude and love.

We thank Horizon and its staff for pointing us to the sustainability path. In particular, Katie Hughes and Sherif Nadar who repeatedly urged and questioned us over the relevance and meaning of sustainability, encouraging us to research more deeply into it to go beyond the hype.

Tinya Yang and Jonathan Fisher were instrumental in making us recognise this was something worth publishing. Julia Hoskins, Charlotte Merritt, and many others helped by contributing their own reflections. David's sister Teresa was key in introducing us to many people who helped us along the way, and Regina for helping us to find a publisher.

We thank in particular Andrew Sheng, Takafumi Sato, Jamil Anderlini, Erkki Liikanen, and Kamiar Mohaddes for the opportunities they gave for us to express our thoughts. In particular, Kamiar and the staff at King's College, Cambridge for providing us with the opportunity to speak on the subject and the many people who helped us with it.

Finally, everything is possible when we have the support of others. Francisco Riviera, Rachel Ganz, Cerian Price, Andrew Zachary, Silvia Flesia, Polly Shaw, and Koo Dahinden provided this for us at the very beginning – before the book was even an idea. They are the foundation to Rethinking Choices.

Contents

CHAPTER 1:

THE SUSTAINABILITY MYTH

We need to educate ourselves better and make the choices ourselves.

Our actions are not insignificant – they matter.

Sustainability is now a major commercial industry.

Even with the Coronavirus raging in 2020, $288 billion went into sustainable investments globally. Despite this being a year when people were losing jobs and the general economic outlook was gloomy, this amount of investments is double the amount that went into it in 2019, and this phenomenal pace of growth is set to accelerate in the years to come.

Larry Fink, the CEO of BlackRock, one of the largest investment companies, wrote an open letter in January 2021 addressed to all the CEOs in the world. In the letter, he reiterated how urgent it is for businesses to do their part, highlighting all the points that we have heard in the media: the crisis is upon us; we need urgent action; businesses need to look to new technologies and to make genuine efforts to change their practices; those businesses which have already made the change have been rewarded with a *sustainability premium* and tremendous opportunities are still available for those willing to make the transition.

In the past few years, the investment industry has been transformed into a huge machine promoting sustainable investments. What started some time ago as a call for caution has now switched to a call for an accelerated investment transition. Larry Fink's letter is part of BlackRock's own promotion in this regard, and the crux of the message is that there is a huge amount of money to be made in 'saving the planet'.

The stock market outperformance of some of these companies with a *sustainability premium* has been truly out of this world. Tesla, for example, became 10 times more valuable over the course of one year, namely 2020, propelling its founder Elon Musk to becoming one of the wealthiest men on earth. It is now the world's most highly priced car maker and is worth more than all the other car makers put together.

The future of the climate, though, is just as uncertain as it was a year ago. The amount of greenhouse gas emission may have abated a little over 2020, but that was due to the Coronavirus and not because of the 10-fold rise in the value of the electric-vehicle manufacturing company. Tesla's much higher share price has not meant climate change is solved, nor does it mean that it will be solved. It just means that someone made a lot of money on the back of our good intentions.

In fact, whenever we see investments make such outsized returns, they tend to result in something horrible happening to our world. According to its annual report, Tesla now has so much cash that it divested $1.5 billion into bitcoin. This has given bitcoin a new lease of life by more or less doubling the price of the currency to $50,000 a bitcoin. Bitcoin funds ransomware attacks; this is where cyber attackers hijack an organisation's data by encrypting it and demanding a ransom payment for the decryption key. It is one of its main commercial uses, if not its only commercial use. When its value goes up, profits to the data hijackers go up and the incentive to make more ransomware attacks goes up. When we bid up the value of Tesla by such a large amount that the company runs out of ways to spend its cash, it ends up risking more ransomware attacks for the rest of us by driving up the price of bitcoin.

This is the way the financial markets work.

With more money, especially ridiculously large amounts of it, we do not get purposeful investments that help to save our planet. Instead, what happens are more nice-sounding investments into poor-quality opportunities that seek fast returns. If the number of ransomware attacks increases, then more companies will be held ransom, and they will need more bitcoin to rescue their data. Bitcoin, legitimised by illegal activities, will become in demand. So there may be a greater need for bitcoin and a higher value for the cryptocurrency. Others seeing Tesla's interests will see this as a signal that cryptocurrencies are getting a nod of approval from not only one of the world's largest car manufacturers but also one that is identified with the message of saving the planet. More people will follow its example and boost up the price of bitcoin further.

Tesla may be buying cryptocurrency to cover the cost of potential ransom demands. It may be buying bitcoin to benefit from an increase in the price of the cryptocurrency, even if that is driving more ransomware attacks. The chicken or the egg? It does not matter which comes first, all that matters is that it is a cycle with profits to be made. This is the way financial markets work.

It does not end here. As the value of bitcoin increases, other activities are dragged into competing with it purely based on returns, and legitimate businesses which cannot produce the same magnitude of performances ultimately suffer. In the end, no business which is valued on the basis of providing a good, strong, and steady income to its owners can compete against the meteoric rise in value that is possible only from speculative flights of fancy.

Bitcoin, incidentally, is produced through a computer algorithm and requires a vast amount of computing resources. Basically, each bitcoin is like a special number in the set of all numbers. They have special properties which make them identifiable as bitcoin. To search for one is like looking for prime numbers among the sea of numbers, and when we find one that has not been found previously, we can lay claim to it as our own. The way we can be sure we have a genuine bitcoin and it is ours, and it has not been claimed already, is for its entire record of ownership to be kept in a way that it cannot be faked.

So, to make sure of this, every bitcoin's ownership history is stored across many, many computers. The idea is that it will literally take more computing resources than anyone has, or any organisation can afford to have, to corrupt and fake the history of all the transactions that have been made. This way, when we find a bitcoin, we can check against the databases and verify whether the bitcoin we have just discovered is genuinely new or not. The databases are therefore vast, globally located, and constantly growing.

Cambridge University has calculated the amount of electricity needed to maintain bitcoin each year. It currently runs to more than the total energy consumed by a country like the Netherlands. This amount of energy alone can power all the *always-on* but inactive devices in the US for almost two years, and for those of us who like tea, it can also provide the UK with sufficient energy to boil its kettles for 27 years. To power all this and keep the process profitable, bitcoin miners who are the people who process the computer algorithm looking for the next special number have joined up with coal miners to generate electricity cheaply. Each successive bitcoin is significantly harder than the previous one to find; if looking for the first is like looking for a needle in a haystack, looking for the next bitcoin is like looking for a needle in all the haystacks in the world, and looking for the one after is like looking for it in the entire galaxy. So, in addition to the energy used to run the data centres, we need a lot of cheap energy to find more bitcoins; therefore, coal mines that have been closed because of the transition to clean energy are now being reopened. To feed this bitcoin habit, we may be burning coal for electricity for a long time.

While we own shares in Tesla because we want to save the planet from climate change, its management team is investing in an asset that is used to pay ransom to data hijackers and causes as much greenhouse gas emission as a country the size of New Zealand while reopening coal mines we have worked hard to shut. All this is our own doing because we are the owners of the electric car company and the management team, in principle, works for us.

If we are gloating over the phenomenal returns from our investment choices, we are demonstrating that 'our left hand simply does not know what our right hand is doing'.

However, even if we do know this, we accept it because we have to. We have ourselves and our families to feed and financial obligations to meet. For those of us who are caught in the sandwich generation, our days flip between worrying about care for our elderly parents and supporting our children growing up. If we are close to our own retirements, we also have fears over our financial future. We cannot live without money and investments, and we depend on our economic system. We need our growth.

Of course, sustainability matters and because of this Larry Fink's letter is an easy sell. Pick a topic that everyone agrees on and advocate increasing investments that promise to prevent catastrophes and offer a new future and higher returns, and preach it boldly from a moral high ground – how can we not follow?

However, there will not be the win-win scenarios that Larry Fink is suggesting. This book is about the impossible choices we face; the truth will be thought-provoking even if it is uncomfortable.

Why do we bother to get up in the morning? Why do we continue with the 'lather, rinse, repeat' we do every day, especially when the word *repeat* was added to double consumption to increase sales? We need to ask ourselves these questions to understand what we want from our lives. Each one of us has our own answers. They are based on our own sense of individual purpose that guides us and gives our lives meaning. It is a purpose that sustains us from our youth to our old age, from birth to death, through successes and failures, through companionship and loneliness.

Sustainability may be an outcome if we can fulfil this purpose, appreciating that whatever we take is not ours but is taken from someone else, otherwise the sustainable growth that is being offered is nothing but a myth.

We face individual ethical and economic choices. No matter what governments and businesses may do for us or offer us, these choices befall us as individuals to make. Whether we are able to make these choices on the basis of ethics or economics will determine what will happen. We need to be reminded that 'the secret of man's being is not only to live but to have something to live for'. Only then is sustainability a possible outcome.

When we talked about our consumption and growth with our friends, one mentioned a conversation she had with her partner. He commented that if everyone were to cut down on what they spend, we would have no jobs and there would be nothing to consume. That would be disastrous for us and would ultimately be terrible for the planet. While our consumption harms the planet, it still pays for all the efforts expended to protect and nurture it; and while our consumption creates the inequalities we abhor, it still pays for elevating our standard of living, freeing our lives from the pestilences and injustices that were prevalent in the previous centuries.

The earliest paper we found on climate change was by Svante Arrhenius, published in 1896. Titled *On the Influence of Carbonic Acid in the Air upon the Temperature of the Ground*, it is basically about global warming. He points out observations made by earlier researchers that if it were not for the heat-absorbing gases, the earth's temperature would probably fall to -200°C. Greenhouse gases are necessary. Too little and we will freeze, but too much and we will boil.

That is the same with all the things that are causing our sustainability issues. We need them all, but if we have too much of them we will die. We cannot stop what we do without losing something that is important to us, but we cannot continue without risking what is also important to us.

The early literature on the damage we were doing to our planet and our environment focused on individual responsibility. The ideas of 'Reduce, Reuse, and Recycle' were promoted to change how we live on a personal basis. From the 1950s to the 1970s the problems of overconsumption were actively pointed out. There was even a strong call to individuals to stop having children to avoid overpopulation as an act of self-sacrifice for the greater good. It would hurt ourselves and our economies, but that was a price worth paying.

As the evidence of climate change accumulated, the literature moved on to discuss how to improve the narrative to make it more impactful, and storytelling designed to reach us on an emotional level began to replace the drier scientific reporting. As the call for conservation grew, cute animals started to appear. By the time of the Paris Agreement, the focus had shifted further towards government action, and the emphasis on individual responsibility to curb consumption started to fade. These were pitched as big problems that could only be resolved by high-level government intervention.

The Paris Agreement required countries to commit to setting their own targets and taking appropriate actions. As this was developing, the message that there were substantial economic benefits in a new world began to take root. Investing in the new alternatives promised untold riches, and the story started to change from saying we cannot have it all to say we can have it all. The message that we each need to make sacrifices that defined the movements in the 1970s faded into the background and gradually disappeared.

In the current moment, we are seeing an investment shift that is promoting more activities, and this is designed to increase our hopes for the future even as our greenhouse gas emissions continue to rise. The transition we are promised requires money, and we are told to hurry up and invest it. Our money will save the world, but more importantly, we will make more money from it. Our experiences, however, have been very different. Our savings and investments which have increased since the 1970s have made 'making more money' the dominant reason for why we grow, produce, and sell things. We no longer grow, produce and sell things to help us live, but do so to make sure our money continues to grow. All our goods and services have become part of the financialisation of modern life. This financialisation has been very harmful and the financialisation of sustainability is not going to be a good thing.

Good investment ideas do not need greed to become corrupted from their original intents. All that we need is a demand for investment returns that is disconnected from what our world can provide. Our ingenuity will do the rest. We need a high level of investment returns to provide the money we need for our future to support ourselves and our families. The problem is more fundamental than whether we have a sufficiently long-term investment horizon or not, or whether the companies we invest in are using sustainable practices or not. It is simply that 'the maths' does not work out. If we look to investment returns to guarantee our future, then it is our needs that are dictating the level of investment returns required. If we insist on this level of investment returns, then we will have to exhaust our planet's resources to provide them. That is what 'the maths' looks like.

When we say we are moving to sustainable growth, we are proposing that we can increase the capacity of what our planet can provide. It is possible to do this, but it takes time and a lot of experimentation. It does not come about simply because we are putting vast amounts of money into it. Importantly, it will require good science. Investments can help good science to develop, but good science does not happen simply because there is a lot of money put into it. In fact, investing a lot of money is more likely to increase the need for financial profits that will hinder good science from happening.

We need the right kind of patience to wait for good scientific ideas to develop. This is not the patience to wait for returns, which is what the ideas of having longer investment horizons imply. It is patience to allow evidence to speak before we can develop the ideas and then use experiments to test implementations before we rush headlong into creating damaging unintended consequences. This is the kind of patience that accepts we cannot predict the future, and so we cannot know when progress can be made. So, while we wait, we have to re-learn how to live in a world with limited resources.

When we grow by more than 1% per annum, according to research on recycling published in the sustainability journal *SAPIENS*, we are using resources faster than the capacity our planet currently has to replenish them. A 1% growth rate would be considered semi-disastrous for most developed economies and an absolute catastrophe for our pension portfolios. No publicly listed company today would even consider suggesting such a low growth rate as their long-term growth path. No investment manager producing this would have a job left to go back to. Our current savings and investments are looking to make at least 10 times this each year and every year. As the world becomes increasingly dominated by investments, 'the maths' is that we will need to make many more times than the 1% that our planet is capable of providing to support our future.

If it is not clear by now why we need this high return, it is because we need to save for the future. Therefore, each year we need the planet to produce not only enough for us to live through the year, but also enough for each of the future years we are saving for. As we expect to live longer and have greater expectations and needs for the future, our planet needs to provide more and more each year.

We write this book to open up a discussion of what our growth is doing and how our investments impact our world. We look into our choices, how our economic system determines them in one way, and how ethics from the time when people were forced to live with limits can help us. We explore questions about what it means to live with uncertainty about the future and what all this may say about our investments.

Sustainability has taken on the shape of a universal cause; even cluster munition manufacturers have corporate social responsibility action plans that promote it as they advertise the horrible killing power of their products. We cannot rely on businesses and governments to make the world into what we need. Lots of small actions on our part has made the world into what it is, and it will be the small actions on our part that will determine what the world will be.

Q&A

Q: We have got the net-zero carbon plans, the Paris Agreement, sustainable investing, and pretty much every business has a sustainability plan, but the global temperature is still increasing, and all the reports suggest we are not deviating from this trajectory. Each week, we hear about environmental problems everywhere. What are we doing wrong at the moment?

A: We are taking the credit up-front for the sustainable initiatives. We do this because we want all the benefits and are unwilling to take any hit to our own consumption. This means we still have the view that we live in a world of unlimited resources. And hence, from this perspective, sustainability is used to create more activities and make more money, with a vain hope that our actions may work out at some point in the future.

We fall in with this thinking because we accept the messages that it is too big for us to solve individually.

If we genuinely believe we are running out of resources, we will have to accept it is necessary to make sacrifices and stop using what's left of them. However, policymakers and businesses cannot force this on us, so it has to come about individually, through each of us doing the right thing.

CHAPTER 2:

IT'S OUR MONEY, STUPID!

We have saved a lot of money for our retirements, but that is not actually helping our future. We need to think less about retiring and more about how to live as we get older.

In December 2013, *Fortune* magazine published an article titled *This wine brought to you by ... retired teachers*. The article highlights that TIAA-CREF is a substantial vineyard owner in California. TIAA-CREF is an acronym that stands for Teachers Insurance and Annuity Association of America and College Retirement Equities Fund. It is one of the oldest pension funds in the world; started in 1918 to cater to the needs of teachers in America, it once boasted the physicist Albert Einstein as a member. Since then, it has broadened its membership base and is now one of the largest investment managers in the world, looking after the pension investments of millions of people.

Their grapes also go into the wines we drink.

Their foray into agriculture started in 2007 when the prevailing investment theme was diversification. Traditionally, pension managers invested the money placed under their care by making so-called stock market investments by buying and selling shares in *public companies*, which are also known as *listed companies*. These are the companies that manufacture the everyday products we use: foods, office and household goods, cars, trucks, and more. They are also the larger shops and restaurant chains, online businesses, major banks, and construction companies. Typically, they have a global reach, and each one is worth tens of billions of US dollars with the larger ones like Apple and Microsoft worth trillions of US dollars.

When the pension managers use our money to buy their shares, we become owners giving us the right to a share in their earnings. When we make these investments, we are investing in the *equity* of the companies, that is, the residual value after all the debt and liabilities have been accounted for. We benefit financially when the companies perform well through increased revenues or through increased share price which gives us the opportunity to sell at a higher price to make a profit. However, if the companies fail to meet their liabilities and go bankrupt, our ownership becomes worthless.

Regulations exist to ensure that the businesses are legitimate, enforcing disclosure requirements so that all relevant information is available publicly. This ensures a minimum quality of financial control. Pension funds are particularly attracted to stock market investments because of the assured minimum quality and because the large size of the companies allows for large investments to be made.

A company that makes its shares available for public trading benefits by having a better profile and this, in turn, enhances its image and standing and improves among other things its credit rating. This gives it better access to funding for different projects it may wish to take on. As a result, when pensions started to invest in public companies, the companies followed by making themselves more attractive to pensions as investments. However, they did this not just by making their products better, but by changing their financial structure so that they appeared more profitable without having to alter their products and sales, such as through more automation to reduce their costs or relocating where their revenues were registered to reduce their tax liabilities. As this went on, the prices for the shares became driven as much, if not more, by how a company structured its finances as by what it was producing.

One by one, much like competitors in a beauty pageant, different companies mimicked each other to achieve similar performances as they strove to compete for our investments. If one company discovered an advantage by relocating its activities to reduce its tax liabilities, other companies promptly followed. This process is called financialisation where financial interests dominate over genuine purpose, and the result is irrespective of what business a company might be in, its performance became very similar to that of all the others.

Pension funds, therefore, looked beyond companies for opportunities that were not as influenced by financialisation. The real economy was an obvious choice. This is the economy of tangible activities rather than financial activities. For example, a farmer growing crops and selling them are tangible activities, while lending money to the farmer is a financial activity. So investing in crops is investing in the real economy, and investing in the bank that lends money to the farmer is investing in the financial economy. In these real businesses, there is little opportunity for financial shenanigans, and the profits are directly related to the actual production of goods. Moving into these areas was intended to make our pension investments more stable, hence the term diversification, but it ended up making the real economy more fragile. As our real economy became more fragile, our planet became less sustainable.

The fact that there was a need to move into the real economy should have been a warning. Our savings and investments had grown to a size that our economy was simply not growing fast enough to provide the returns they were needing. What should have been recognised and is still not recognised is that we needed to accept less return for our savings and investments. With lower returns, however, we will not have enough money in our pensions to allow us to retire or to pay for our care when we are elderly.

Pension funds venturing into agriculture made sense from a portfolio perspective, but the size of our real economy is significantly smaller than the size of our financial economy. So, if our savings and investments were already swamping the financial economy, the real economy stood no chance. All the same, when returns are necessary, anything which can provide a steady stream of income cannot be ignored. Agriculture is ideal for providing a steady stream of income. Food is something that we always need, and mechanisation and technology will allow farms to keep producing. Marketing can always be relied on to introduce people to new products and tastes so that more produce can be sold.

Pineapples, for example, can be sliced and sold in small packs for a lunch snack as a different product from the whole fruit, and a new market niche will be created. Whatever is grown will be marketed and sold, and even if the produce is not eaten, the excess can be passed on as recyclable fuel for energy. With this relabelling nothing goes to waste, and agribusinesses can keep producing more without it being seen as excessive; we can have the returns we need for our retirement.

The December 2017 issue of *Wine Business Monthly* lists the top 100 vineyard owners in Napa Valley, one of California's premier wine regions. This is compiled using a mix of public records, direct queries to the vineyard owners, and data from the magazine's own proprietary database. At the top of the list are Treasury Wine Estates, TIAA/Silverado Investment Management Co, and Constellation Brands.

Constellation Brands and Treasury Wine Estates are *listed companies*. These companies are global; the first is American, the second is Australian. Constellation Brands is over 85% owned by mutual funds, which are funds provided by companies like Fidelity, BlackRock, Vanguard, T Rowe Price, and other household names for us to put our savings and pension investments into. The top 10 shareholders of Treasury Wine Estates are similarly mutual and pension funds. A further proportion of ownership in these companies comes from those of us who manage stock investments themselves. Basically, we as individuals are the majority owners of these companies, holding almost *all* of the shares.

Another way in which ownership of these companies passes through to us is via governments. For example, in Norway, the Norwegian parliament passed a law in 1990 requiring the government to save part of their oil revenue from the North Sea as annual contributions in the same way that we as individuals make regular contributions to our pensions, to build up a national savings fund for the current and future generations. They set up a fund, Norges Bank Investment Management, especially for this and the first money went into it in 1996. It has since grown to be one of the world's largest social savings funds, valued at about $1 trillion and is another big owner of wine businesses. TIAA-CREF, in comparison, also has about $1 trillion under its care.

There are even larger investment managers. The Vanguard Group has $6.2 trillion in assets under management as of January 2020 and has over 30 million investors. It is also among the top 10 shareholders of the Treasury Wine Estates. The individual accounts of their 30 million investors, however, vary greatly in size. Vanguard Group's 2019 *How America Saves* report gives the statistics that half of the accounts have less than $22,217 in them, while the average account size is $92,148.

PWC is one of the major international business consultancy groups, and it regularly surveys and reports on different industries. Its *Asset Management 2020* report estimated global investment assets at $101.7 trillion. This is *our* money, 'our' being pretty much everyone in the developed world. Through our pensions, college funds, rainy day savings, and social security funds, we are the world's capital owner.

Having this much money is a problem, especially for the sustainability of our world. The savings reflect that we are increasingly looking to a pot of money to cover any future uncertainty. The problem with this is that money is not always able to do that. First of all, you need to have enough money. Second, some things may not be best covered with money. If we fall ill, the money may help us get treatment, but saving for potential treatment we may or may not need is not as effective as spending the money now to prevent falling ill. Still, we are urged constantly to save and because we do not know how much we may need, reaching for the highest return on our savings is the only thing to do. All this is bad news for sustainability.

Schroeder, another investment company, published a *2020 Global Investor Survey*. In the report, it points out what individuals from countries across the world as widespread as Japan, China, Indonesia, the US, Argentina, Brazil and 26 more are expecting as an annual return from their savings. Investors from half of the 32 countries surveyed are expecting a return of over 10.93%. That is, if they had $10,000 at the start of the year, they expect this to grow to $11,093 by the end of the year. At the top of the expectation ranking, investors from the US are on average looking for an annual return of 15.38%, and at the bottom, Japanese investors were satisfied with an annual return of 5.96%.

Applying the 10.93% return expected to the $101.7 trillion of assets means we are expecting our savings to grow by more than

$11 trillion a year. This is about the size of the combined GDP of Germany, the UK, France and Italy. GDP measures the financial value of all our activities: good ones like saving people's lives in our hospitals, poets giving readings, entertaining friends and families; and bad ones like paying bribes in our businesses, promoting drug and gambling addiction, and polluting our environment with excessive travel. We expect our investments to make each year an amount equal to the total money we spend in all activities across these four countries. This works out also to be about twice the total annual salaries of all the workers in these countries. We are expecting that our investments will capture as much money as profits.

The total pension assets in OECD countries have doubled between 2008 and 2018, while the size of our economies measured in GDP has only increased by 30% in the same period; pension assets in the US now accounts for 80% of its economy, up from 30% in 1980. The United Kingdom, Switzerland, Australia, Iceland and the Netherlands all have pension assets worth more than the size of their economies. This means in each of these countries there is more saved for retirements than what is spent in the whole country each year, and it is still not enough.

We actually own this money and before we go further, this also means that the classic demarcation between capital owners and labourers no longer applies. While we still like to protest against 'capital owners' for their exploitation of labour, recognising ourselves as the 'exploited labourers', we are actually the capital owners. Everything that businesses are doing which we complain about is being done to benefit our investments.

Back to the wine.

Grapes in the Old World are traditionally *dry farmed*. That is, irrigation is not used and the fruit grows by the plant drawing moisture from the ground in which the vine is grown. Wine is supposed to taste of the region it comes from: the composition of the soil, the weather, and the flavour of the grape variety. All this magic is captured in that connoisseur term *terroir*, which is the spiritual essence behind the quality control in the French certification of *Appellation d'Origine Contrôlée*. This works because vine roots grow deep, most roots reaching three to four metres into the ground while some might even extend as deep as nine metres. The roots draw whatever humidity there is in the soil, which may come from natural rainfall, rivers and streams, or from underground water. The extensive root system captures highly localised differences in the soil makeup and moisture, and the plants, through the actions of the particular amounts of sunlight and temperature, produce the tastes that make up the *terroir*. This creates an enormous range of characters for the final product, making wine both commonly available and highly prestigious.

The production of wine in this dry-farmed way does not require much more than the natural rainwater that falls on the vineyards. Dry farming, however, as environmental scientist Casey Walsh describes in *Water to Wine*, requires the vines to be placed less densely and varieties that are adapted to the limits of natural precipitation. The vine grower does not call the shots, nature does. That is why each year the vintage is different.

When the vineyards were family owned, as they traditionally had tended to be, the land and the vines were a heritage asset to be managed in perpetuity for all generations. Making wine and selling wine provided the income that allowed the business to continue. There may be a poor year or two, but the wine that was laid down in previous years would help to survive through those. What was important was to care for the land and the plants so that they were never damaged.

For businesses, however, what matters is the profit each year and specifically, the profit should not drop but rather grow. The land is only as valuable as what it can be sold for, and the value is a multiple of the value of the grapes sold in recent years. The most beneficial crop is therefore the grape with the highest current market value and not the ones that work best with the land. To deal with the problem of inconsistent rainfall, since the grapes planted are no longer necessarily the ones most suitable to the climate, agribusinesses rely on technology to smooth out the randomness of nature. It uses irrigation by extracting groundwater to ensure that even in drought seasons, the vines produce exactly what they are calculated to produce. Technology is the magic we use to subvert our planet's natural restrictions.

This is the way in which our savings impact the world we live in, but all this comes at a cost. In the 4.5 billion-year history of the planet, progress has been phenomenal. Starting from space rock, life somehow got a foothold and as organisms discovered their niches, it has enabled other forms of life gradually to appear and help each other in an otherwise barren environment. All this has been through unguided, patient, and open-minded experimentation; trying, testing, and little by little progressing when it led to a healthier whole. The result is a growth rate that cannot be measured with our modern economic targets.

From barren rock to an immensely rich planet, surviving through five mass extinctions from exogenous causes, and all this without at any point risking its own destruction. It has been possible because the planet's natural cycles and restrictions have the patience to allow life to come together in a way that helps each other, without having to know or to measure how much each or the whole is worth financially. In some periods it flourishes and in other periods it regresses, but given enough time it gets richer. If we let the vines grow naturally, they would still produce for us but just not at the constant pace our investments demand.

Today, California has a significant wine industry. In 2019, the estimated retail value of Californian wine in the US was in excess of $43 billion. It produced more than 240 million cases of wine, employing about 6,000 growers, and contributed $3.2 billion of revenue to them. To keep this running, for one gallon of wine an estimated average of 318 gallons of water for irrigation is used. Given that rainfall is highly unpredictable, and without it, the yield of the crop can vary quite substantially, this irrigation helps the grower to manage the uncertainties around nature.

California provides the US with a third of its vegetables and two-thirds of its fruits and nuts. In the State's 2018-2019 *Agricultural Statistics Review*, grapes and almonds followed dairy in the top three positions for their contributions. To keep this industry going, California pumps the most groundwater of any state in the US, using it mostly for irrigation. Even though almonds, like grapes, are also traditionally dry-farmed, irrigation helps to achieve the highest yield possible, independently of climate conditions. TIAA-CREF, by carefully measuring and controlling nature, is acting in our best interest to ensure the best returns for our investments.

The use of groundwater is, however, really troublesome. Surface water comes from rain, snow and other forms of precipitation from the atmosphere. This flows into lakes, rivers and eventually out to sea where it is evaporated by the heat from the sun, and the cycle continues. Along the way, plants also take up the water and transpire it back to the atmosphere, as we draw ours from the streams, rivers and lakes. Groundwater comes partly from this contribution, where surface water filters deep into the ground, but a lot of it comes from underground lakes that have been in existence for a very long time. A healthy level of groundwater can help to maintain the level of rivers and streams in dry seasons. In some places, this water also helps to hold the ground up, literally. Along coastal regions, groundwater can keep salt water from intruding.

In California, for some time now, so much groundwater has been drawn that natural rainfall and melting snow can no longer replenish it; surface water in rivers and streams has dried up; saltwater has been intruding into coastal regions. Substantial subsidences have also occurred in areas where aquifers have been emptied causing the ground to sink. In 2014, the *Sustainable Groundwater Management Act* was passed in California to deal with this. It is a bit like the Paris Agreement for climate change in recognising that there is a serious problem that needs the co-operation of many parties.

The act established a series of 260 local Groundwater Sustainability Agencies, each charged to develop its own Groundwater Sustainability Plan to manage the future of groundwater in its regions. The plans were required to be submitted for approval, or the regions risked state intervention and control. Of the water basins, 127 were considered requiring high- or medium-priority action, and these regions accounted for 96% of the water drawn. The agencies responsible for these regions were given until the beginning of 2020 to come up with their Groundwater Sustainability Plan and were then required to follow their stated paths to stabilise their groundwater levels by 2040.

For some, like North Kings, the plan is a continued reduction in the amount of groundwater it draws over the coming decade with an estimate that the groundwater will stabilise at no deeper than 170 feet below ground. As a comparison, this is 15 feet worse than the level in 2017 and 45 feet worse than the level in 1991.

A May 2020 review by the Public Policy Institute of California (PPIC) on the 36 management plans proposed by the agencies in the San Joaquin Valley, the state's largest agricultural region, noted that only 20% of the actions involved adjusting water demand. Adjustments may be made by changing how agriculture is done, such as with land fallowing or by direct pumping restrictions. The rest of the plans relied on the natural recharge of the aquifers; that is, waiting or hoping for sufficient rain, and potential gains from water recycling and wastewater management. Basically, with only 20% focused on adjusting water demand, the emphasis is on no change in what we do. The plans become a way for the farmers to legitimise doing the same.

Ellen Hanak, the director of the PPIC, emphasised the one takeaway of their review: without anything in place to make sure it all adds up to a net benefit, chances are that everyone will think they are doing the right thing, but together the problem will continue and worsen.

In many ways, with our investments managed on our behalf by TIAA-CREF and similar asset managers, we are guilty of the same. Each manager may be doing the best in terms of sustainability. However, because our assets are so large and our demand for returns is so strong, there is nothing to say that this will not continue to drive competition and consumption beyond what is sustainable.

CHAPTER 3:

A DEAL WITH THE DEVIL

We can't just do what makes us feel good. A
path to a genuinely purposeful life will force us
to go beyond our comfort zone and will cost us.

The British Broadcasting Corporation (BBC) reported in August 2019 about a family who moved to northern Lapland as their personal response to climate change. They live a natural, outdoor life. The report shows them next to a pristine lake, so clean that the water can be drunk directly. In winter, they have to cut through the ice for water. They feed themselves by fishing, hunting, and keeping poultry and sheep. They also have a sauna for personal hygiene. Their children still attend school, and they remain connected with the modern world.

They benefit from occasional edible but marked out-of-date produce from supermarkets which their friends bring when they visit. Their nearest supermarket is over 100 kilometres away. They laugh about how stupid it is for tomatoes grown in Senegal, packed in France, in plastic, of course, to be sold in Ivalo and end up being cast away by supermarkets in northern Lapland so that their friends can pick up the vegetables for them.

Janne Utriainen, the father of the family, has this to say:

> They think that we can solve replacing the fossil fuels with solar, or wind energy, or something. That's nonsense. We don't solve the problem by changing things, by recycling things. We solve the thing by not doing the things.

The family is fortunate to have a place in northern Lapland where they can genuinely 'not do the things'. Not many of us can do that. What is more, if a billion of us were to follow their example – that is, go to our nearest equivalent of a pristine wilderness – the result would be devastating. First, the remaining pieces of unspoilt nature left around us would be destroyed, and secondly, there would be no one left to bring the out-of-date produce from the supermarkets.

More seriously though, the way our economic system has come to be organised, such a move would be a disaster. With no one left manning the shops or mending the roads, the support of our core infrastructures would disappear. Shops would not get stocked as delivery drivers would be busy building huts in the woods, road accidents would not be attended to, and hospitals would be empty of staff but probably full of newly motivated survivalists seeking emergency treatment for injuries. Even Janne and his family would have to give up on their friends visiting.

Our lives are organised to serve and to be served by a common infrastructure that provides us with all the benefits we enjoy and has facilitated all the progress that we have made. Without it, modern society would cease to function.

Our economy works in a way that does not let us 'not do the things'. It is a network of uncountably many loose connections that is impossible to unravel. When we hold back from doing one thing, other things adjust to compensate. We cannot simply say, "let's not do this bit" and expect that to mean we have cut back. We may think that being vegan means there will not be any more deforestation, but it may be that the land becomes more valuable as a result of the crops being directly used for human consumption rather than for animal feed, and drive more speculation and development.

When we turn off our mobile phones in an effort to reduce electricity consumption, electricity will still be used to keep cell towers working so that we can reconnect at speed and have our profiles updated. It may also justify more spending on the vast satellite networks for mobile phones we are sending up at the moment, just so that we can reconnect better and faster, perhaps also prompting handset upgrades that will make our turning on and off more convenient. Even when we try not to consume, our society's demands on resources grow to make it convenient for us to 'not consume'.

Car transport is a major user of fossil fuel, but during the Coronavirus crisis we still used about 85 million barrels of oil per day. This was even though an estimated 3.9 billion people or half of the world's population were locked down and most of us were working from home and not commuting. That is a reduction of only 15% from the pre-lockdown level and is about the level we were using back in 2008. Instead of us travelling ourselves, the delivery vans which were making sure our online orders arrived were doing the travelling and the consumption for us. The increase in internet usage, the added heating in our homes, the extra toilet paper we were flushing down our residential toilets, all these were parts of the consumption chain which we would not have wanted to or could not reduce.

This 'not doing', which is very easy to talk about, is something very difficult, if not impossible, for society as a whole to achieve.

During the Coronavirus pandemic, we still needed to keep our businesses going. As the lockdown progressed, each and every government turned their messages to the economy, and at times and in certain countries it became a case of 'the economy' versus 'the people'. We need consumption. To keep up consumption we need people to stay employed. To keep people employed, we need to keep up corporate earnings. To keep up corporate earnings, we need to keep up consumption.

Governments too need income. To keep the governments with income, we need taxes, so we need people to be employed for income tax, corporates to keep up earnings for corporation tax, and consumption to continue for value-added tax. This tax money is used to provide the support of the common infrastructure that keeps the whole society functioning.

The Coronavirus pandemic interrupted this by killing some people and making others sick. With work disrupted, consumption stopped, earnings stopped, the economy keeled over, government finances collapsed, and the common support to restart was put at risk. We saw the costs of stopping this cycle in the increase in inequalities and hardships, and for all that cost, it translated to a meagre 15% reduction in our oil consumption. If we want to keep inequalities and hardships at bay, our economy is telling us we need to keep 'doing the things'. Reducing is not an option.

Unfortunately, we do more than just keep 'doing the things'. Because the way growth works is that with each cycle, more is actually needed to be done than in the cycle before; otherwise it is not growth, it is stagnation. Changing how we do things, as Janne observed, does not alter this, it just changes where the impact of what we do will be felt.

We are already seeing this. Investigations by an EU funded project, Danwatch, revealed the impact of the nascent switch to electric vehicles. In 2019, we sold 2.1 million electric cars versus a total global car production of 73 million. That is barely 3% of the total production. However, even with this small amount, the costs can already be seen.

According to reports, Chile has been the producer of over 40% of the lithium used in batteries in the past two decades. Electric vehicles create additional demand for this lithium. The push for this is hurting local communities with the typical sidelining of their interests by mining companies and governments, and has permanently desiccated parts of their environment through heavy water and brine use. Chile is not the only country affected. Bolivia has significant reserves, allegedly the largest accessible ones in the world.

The 2019 Bolivian election which overthrew Evo Morales triggered speculations about capitalist interests interfering with the political process. America, obviously, was the suggested bogeyman, but German companies and Chinese interests also featured. Lithium access is becoming an issue of national security for every country. From back in 2009, Morales was an advocate for keeping these resources nationally and for the indigenous Indians from whose land the lithium would eventually be mined. The subsequent interim president, Jeanine Añez, was in favour of transferring the resources to private hands. She was suspended soon after her election as she was held responsible for the massacre of protesters; the Bolivian Senate recently recommended her trial on charges of genocide and other crimes. As usual, money always seems to find a way to become connected with political misdemeanours. Elon Musk, the CEO of Tesla and so had its impeccable green credentials behind him, tweeted (and since deleted), "We will coup whoever we want! Deal with it."

Such tension is already developing when we have barely begun the electrification of the vehicle parc. Given the complexity of the economy, one man's good is another's evil. If we cannot stop doing things, all our responsible and green intentions will not prevent substantial harm from happening.

A research group at the School of Sustainability at Arizona State University researched the impact of lithium mining. They found a paucity of papers addressing this issue. Our pattern has always been to grow until we can grow no further. Only at that point, when some limit has been severely breached, does our creativity turn towards fixing things or seeking alternatives. The paucity of papers suggests we may need to grow further before attention properly turns to the damage we are creating.

This brings Janne's comment to life. A transformation to electric vehicles is good and makes us feel good, so we rush into it, legitimised by the message that it will solve our climate change problems, but we are blind to the possibility that we are simply pushing the issues somewhere else. This will continue until the problem becomes big enough to limit further transition.

In the space of a few thousand years, we have come from having to suffer the randomness of death through diseases to having a pretty much predictable life span. We now have better clothing, better food, better health, and even greater varieties of entertainment than not only our ancestors of several thousand years back but even ourselves had a decade or so ago. All this is possible because we have been making deals with an economic system where we accept the need to keep growing as a trade-off for the benefits offered. However, as our economy has become more and more complex, this has become a deal with the devil where there is always a cost.

There is no easy way. Genuine sustainability cannot come without 'not doing', and for that, we have to pay a cost. Equally, the deal with the devil that lets us keep doing also has a price, and the payment date for that is fast catching up with us.

CHAPTER 4:

ONCE IN A LIFETIME – WELL... HOW DID I GET HERE?

Breaking things into tiny little transactions
makes us lose sight of what we are living for
and encourages us to mistreat the world.
It's the whole that counts.

We need to keep purpose in mind, even in the
small things we do.

Once in a Lifetime is a song by Talking Heads. It was released in 1980 and the vocalist, David Byrne, is seen in the official music video as a preacher giving a sermon. The song depicts an image of us waking up one day in surprise to find our lives full of trophies and asks:

And you may find yourself behind the wheel of a large automobile

And you may find yourself in a beautiful house, with a beautiful wife

And you may ask yourself, "Well... how did I get here?"

This chapter takes us through the history and development of some of the economic ideas we now take for granted. We explore how psychology, marketing, business and politics all play their part in turning concepts into the received wisdom and how these concepts enable us to replace ethical considerations to support our pursuits, especially that of money.

To start, we look at the idea of growth. Economics does not answer why we need to grow. It accepts it as self-evidently true that we will always prefer more to less.

When I first started in the investment industry, the firm I joined had an introductory week of training to bring all the new starters up to date. It was a prestigiously intellectual firm, headed by top academics, policymakers, and market savvy traders with pretty much everyone having at least one doctorate degree. The week of training included courses to cover the practical aspects of our work. There was quite a lot of quantitative and mathematical materials that explained the whys and wherefores of what it was that we did and how we did it. The company was an investment fund, and what we did was to buy things cheaply to sell them later for a profit when the prices adjusted.

The job of the new starters was to implement technology to look through all the possible opportunities and to identify the ones which were mispriced so that the investment managers could get on with the buying. The aim was to capture everything and leave nothing on the table. The reason was that if we did not exploit all the opportunities, then someone else would. So if the opportunities would be exploited anyway, it made sense that we should be the ones to get to them first for the good of ourselves and of our investors.

Leaving nothing on the table is a reflection of the idea of preferring more to less. Our investors would have been disappointed in us and we would not have done our job if we had not preferred more ourselves but had left something on the table for others. However, the actual economic idea of preferring more to less is more subtle. It is that we prefer more utility, that is, a more useful and purposeful life. Lifetime utility, which is what economics says we should care about, is about being able to look back in our old age and ask whether we would be able to face death with wisdom and integrity, or with despair. This utility is almost impossible to model mathematically, and so in economic textbooks, it is simplified into exercises that focus on maximising money. Maximising money then becomes the *de facto* accepted goal of what we should do with our lives.

We see again and again cases where the depth of an original idea is lost but the simplification lives on. In this case, the economic idea that we should live full and wholesome lives is lost, while the idea of seeking the most money survives. Over time, with each repetition the status of this simplification is elevated further and further until it becomes a fundamental and irrefutable 'truth', and we end up with ideas of 'leave nothing on the table', and 'more money is always better'.

However, when we take everything from the table and leave nothing for others, then all we have left is a sustainability problem.

The truth is we do want more and to understand why we want more and what we want more of, we need to turn to psychology. In 1943, Abraham Maslow published a paper titled *Theory of Human Motivation*. He was a psychologist and was innovative in his time for researching the workings of the mind. By focusing on the 'normal' mind, his work remains significantly relevant to us even today. In his paper, he pointed out, "Man is a perpetually wanting animal." The important word here is 'perpetually'. It means we are never sated. We want things, and if ever a 'want' is satisfied, we will want something else. Maslow expressed this in terms of a hierarchy of needs, where each level of need is revealed in the types of things we want. This is the reason why we have always been and will always be striving for more. It is also why marketing is so successful because we naturally want. This explains why our economies are in this cycle of consumption and why growth is such a natural concept to accept. Everyone is perpetually motivated by 'want'.

Any proposal for sustainability that presumes we will be satisfied in a utopian paradise where we will no longer want is simply not going to work. This also means we will always be growing.

Imagine we are in a perfect world where everything is to our liking. At some point, we will feel a desire to have something different, even something so trivial as, say, a different shape for our bread. If we follow this up, then we will create a change to make the bread in a different shape. Others seeing this may also like it and want the same. We may now need a different baking tray. We have responded to a psychological need for something new, and resources have become involved. So even in this perfect world, wanting something different has led to change, and as change is created, growth happens.

In Maslow's hierarchy of needs, the most elemental needs are the physiological ones of which hunger is the most basic. This is hunger to the point of starvation when you literally are not able to think of anything else but food. When someone is at this point of starvation, the need for food motivates every action, and all other desires become suppressed. When we manage to get something to eat, our need for food becomes somewhat sated, and a new level of need kicks in to promote new wants. According to Maslow, the next level of need encompasses safety needs: shelter, physical security, and the like.

When the physiological needs have been sufficiently met, psychological needs emerge. At the lowest level of these are love needs, such as our need for affection and belongingness. Esteem needs are next in the level after that; they are our need for a stable, high evaluation of ourselves and for self-respect. Finally, at the peak of the hierarchy is what Maslow termed self-actualisation. This is the need to express our talents and potentials and is met with creative outlets such as performing art, being inventive, and expressing cleverness.

Needs at different levels can appear simultaneously; the lower level needs do not have to be fully sated before higher level needs emerge. We generally find that we experience a mixture of needs from different levels of the hierarchy at the same time and this is expressed as feelings for a variety of wants. The more basic physiological needs drive our survival, and the higher psychological needs drive our pursuit for growth.

This hierarchy is considered universal and shared by everyone. Maslow, however, also stated there is one further level of need, "to know and to understand", which may be found in some people and not in others. This is the need for things like advanced learning, scientific inquiry, and philosophy. If it is present in a person, it is expressed when all the other needs have been sufficiently satisfied. As you are reading this, you are satisfying this particular need.

Our psychology with its levels of needs is why we perpetually want things, but perpetually wanting things does not equate to 'leaving nothing on the table'. However, even if we were to leave something on the table individually, the rationale of the firm I joined is true and someone else will come and take it. This realisation led Thomas Robert Malthus, back in 1798, to note that society will grow until we run out of resources to grow further.

Malthus wrote *An Essay on the Principle of Population* to counter the proposals at the time of alternative economic systems that would ensure universal fairness. He made the point that all evidence at this time pointed to the fact that society grew until the growth could no longer be sustained and dismissed suggestions that resources could be made to be perpetually available. He argued that if ever additional resources were made available, they would promote another spurt of growth that would stop when resources again became insufficient. He advocated instead the need to accept that we would always be living on the edge of subsistence, and as a result, there would always be some levels of inequality.

For Malthus, society was driven by the physiological need to reproduce and constrained by starvation. In keeping with Maslow's later opinion of man as a perpetually wanting animal, he saw these two drivers in never-ending competition with each other. He stated two laws: "food is necessary to the existence of man" and "the passion between the sexes is necessary and will remain nearly in its present state". Consequently, he concluded, our urge to reproduce would continue and the population would grow until it could no longer be sustained by the amount of food available, no matter how abundant that food might be. His important observation was that growth only stopped when resources became insufficient. In his case, that resource was food. Competition between people at that point meant inequality would always be present, whether by design or by chance, because some people would always find the means to lay claim to more than others. Perfection and absolute equality were therefore impossible.

According to Malthus, however, this was a call to rethink how to better the situation for each other by focusing on improving the production of food. Society would not be stopped simply because growth was stopped. Instead, innovation and creativity would continue, and the "cravings of hunger... will urge man to actions", and our wants would stimulate us to find new ways to grow. He saw society's welfare oscillating between periods of stagnation and misery and growth and wellbeing, depending on whether the food supply was insufficient for everyone or if the means of food production were improved. In the 18th century, this was largely through technology or the conquest of new lands; but equally, he saw growth as coming from the result of diseases, famines, and wars. These reduced the size of the population so that food was once again sufficient. So we grew, either because we had found new ways to do so, or because society had collapsed, opening up new opportunities. These cycles were certain to happen, but they were random and could not be predicted.

Importantly, because these periods of growth and misery could not be predicted, he saw having to live within limits as a necessary outcome. While we may look to expand the planet's capacity, we cannot tell if it will be innovation or pestilence which will provide us with the room to continue our expansion. The Coronavirus pandemic, for example, by having caused businesses to shut down and close, is giving us more room to expand economically when it is over, while the contraction of our economies it caused has also widened our inequalities.

This view is pessimistic to our thinking today. We prefer the view of the sustainability movements that there are solutions that will let us continue forever which stems from our beliefs that technology will always be there to provide solutions.

Malthus was dismissed in his time and still is frequently dismissed as failing to account properly for the power of technological innovations. Around 1850, mechanised farming started to make its mark on agriculture and accelerated in the 1930s with the introduction of the tractor. This massively improved food production and seemingly solved the problems of famine forever. However, the introduction of new technologies brought with it their own problems. The introduction of the tractor brought about the Dust Bowl events in the 1930s with the combination of drought and soil left unprotected, due to larger fields and mechanised farming; this unprotected soil was swept up in winds to become massive dust storms killing livestock and crops. The storms reached above the clouds to a height of two miles and travelled thousands of miles. People developed and died from dust pneumonia. Estimates suggested over 30 million acres of land were rendered useless for farming, and over 100 million more acres rapidly lost their topsoil. The irony of technology was that what started as a solution to increase food production ended by contributing to famine.

Malthus's other assumption, reproduction, also came under attack by technology. Progress in family planning broke the relationship between 'the passion between the sexes' and population size; that is, having sex no longer equated to having children. Technology provided an escape from this cycle of constraints by food, but the reduction in the number of children led to the ageing of our populations and this is contributing to our concerns that we will not be supported in our future. In turn, it is driving our need for high investment returns and is causing the associated impacts on the planet. Technology may have solved one problem, but it also brings about new problems.

The thinking that technology is the answer has been developed into a philosophy of technology solutionism or technology chauvinism. Technology will allow us to keep doing the same thing, and future technology will eventually deal with any damage that current technologies may cause. This legitimises us to continue to live our lives as we do without the need to change what we do. Since this cycle of technology leading to problems that are solved by further technology is a cycle of economic growth, problems are, ultimately, economically beneficial. The bigger the problem, the greater the economic potential. This is the reason why stock markets generally do well when catastrophes happen, as the expectation is that the damage will stimulate more activities, and with more activities, there will be more economic growth. It is also why support for sustainable investing is so strong.

Fossil fuel technology left us with a huge problem, and this is actually a good thing as it offers possibilities for newer technologies to resolve them. It was only when the climate problem took on the narrative of a promise for more economic growth that attention to it really took off. Carbon sequestering, solar farms, drones for tree planting are some of the suggestions of new technologies which have been touted to cure global warming, offering the prospect of a new green economy with unlimited economic prospects. Basically, technology solutions play to the idea that economic growth is always good.

The opposing view that we should not rely on technology is also faulty. The fact is that technology is hugely beneficial and has increased the capacity of our planet to provide for us and improved the ability of our societies to care for each other. However, new technology creates changes, and when the changes happen too rapidly they overrun us and things become unsustainable. As new technologies are discovered, the opportunities for substantial economic gains drive them to be adopted much faster than the knowledge of their impacts and their consequences can be understood. The problem with technological solutions to sustainability and growth is not whether they can be relied on, but whether we believe in them too strongly and adopt them too readily.

Despite having been discredited, Malthus's ideas were far-reaching and in tune with our current debates. He recognised inequality as an inevitable outcome of growth and attacked the focus on activities that did not help to relieve the constraint of resources. At his time, industry was largely for the benefit of the wealthy as most people could not afford manufactured goods. He, therefore, recognised gains from industry as benefitting the capital owners and not contributing to the overall welfare of the population. In his view, only those jobs which enriched the potential of the land for the benefit of all could be considered truly productive. He considered it wrong to pay higher wages for unproductive factory work that only benefitted the wealthy because this attracted labour away from the essential production of food for everyone. This raises questions for us today of whether our scales of pay reflect our collective understanding of productive versus unproductive work, and whether we care about this or not.

As for inequality, he was a disbeliever in the notion that wealth accruing to the higher classes would eventually flow to the rest of the population. This is a prescient rebuke of the 20th century idea of 'trickle-down prosperity', where allowing unfettered room for the wealthy to get richer is considered as the best way to benefit the poor as the rich enable entrepreneurial activities that will benefit everyone. However, this did not make Malthus a modern-day socialist in any sense. He was equally against social measures such as the *poor laws* in England at the time that gave the poor financial help. He considered them evil because they took attention away from addressing the real problem, which was the lack of food, and as a consequence trapped successive generations of the poor into more and more dire situations.

In the case of our world today, the direct cause of the sustainability problem is excessive demands on our planet and our society, but the driver behind those excesses is actually our need for high investment returns. If we want a proper resolution, we have to address the real problem, which is that we are insecure about our own future. We need to learn to face our insecurities and develop ways to support ourselves other than with money.

Malthus considered it essential to include the miseries of those not in the top tier of society in any measure of fairness. In this, he thought that historical accounts were biased in painting too favourable a picture by concentrating on the lives of the wealthy. He looked at the treatment of women as a better indicator of the actual state of society.

He did not give a solution to how we can solve our problems, and this is partly why Malthus is not as recognised today. We prefer solutions. His idea that there are productive and unproductive activities is also at odds with our current idea that all activities are good. We like to think that it is better if we are able to do whatever we want. This brings us to Adam Smith's arguments of the Invisible Hand.

The Invisible Hand is now the most important cornerstone of our capitalist economic foundation. It permits us to grow as fast as we can without requiring any pretence to purpose. It has since been used frequently to justify the individual pursuit of profit as a moral obligation.

At the time when Malthus wrote, Adam Smith had already given a theoretical backing to capitalism through his book *An Inquiry into the Nature and Causes of the Wealth of Nations*. Smith highlighted the division of labour as the "greatest improvements in the productive powers". He gave an example of watching pin-making. He described it as a complex task involving 18 separate steps: drawing the wire, straightening it, cutting, sharpening the point, and so on. A labourer, he said, "uneducated to this business", may manage to make one pin a day. By dividing these tasks between, as he saw on his visits, 10 people, with none of them being particularly skilled in pin-making *per se*, but enabled by machines, they could make 48,000 pins in a day. That is, an improvement of going from one pin per person to 4,800 pins per person. Such was the power of the division of labour.

With the division of labour, workers did not need to be fully skilled anymore. Machines allowed work to be broken down into a collection of menial tasks. In fact, the less skilful the workers were, the better, as they could be paid less. What mattered was how fast they could pick up new tasks. This brought about the need for mass education, and along with it, labour became an exchangeable commodity.

Division of labour separated the worker from the final products they were making. This effectively meant that our work no longer needed to have a recognisable purpose. Think of the days when you might have gone to work in a routine, and having spent the hours fully engaged, to leave at the end of it without any sense of having achieved anything. The only thing that mattered was the final quantity of whatever it was that we were meant to have done.

If our job is to sharpen the pins, it does not matter if the pins are used as the tips of surgical needles for a hospital or as poison darts for a secret police. Our job makes it possible for someone to be saved or to be killed. Once the consideration of the final use is removed from why we work, the only purpose left is our wages. The only thing that matters as to whether someone is killed or is saved is if one paid more than the other. As it is only money that matters, the better paid outcome is therefore the better outcome.

The 18th century was an eventful period of political transitions. In the UK, the century saw the Jacobite uprising to reinstall a monarch. The position of a Prime Minster became established for the first time, and it also saw the last time a monarch, George II, personally leading his country to war. During this period, slavery was abolished in the country, and Britain began to populate the penal colonies in Australia. Further afield, the French Revolution toppled the social hierarchy, and the American Independence wars raged and reversed the status of colony and empire. The South Sea financial crisis broke out, causing widespread financial distress and bankrupted many of the wealthy.

Against such a backdrop, any suggestion that there could be a controller who knew best what to do would have been met with serious ridicule. The Invisible Hand offered an alternative where control was democratised; individuals could simply be left to their own devices and all would be for the greater good.

As long as work is divided into components, and there are open and free markets where such components can be bought and sold, and as long as everyone has sufficient money to participate, supply and demand will do their job and society will flourish. No one needs to be there to guide the whole operation.

The Invisible Hand, however, leaves us with a moral dilemma. Since it is good that we can grow as a society, and the Invisible Hand is the best way to ensure this growth happens, it therefore serves a moral good. If a higher wage allows more growth to happen, then a higher wage has a greater moral good. In this way, profit becomes a tool for moral good. By this argument, if facilitating someone to be killed by secret police pays us better wages, then we will be serving a higher moral good by having our pins used for that. This may seem a facetious argument but it is exactly how it is argued that profit is always good, regardless of how that profit may come about. We may shroud it with comments about how all this has to be within the bounds of legality, but as we have seen and we know all too well, political lobbying and legal obfuscation can make the bounds of legality stretch very far.

The issue with this argument is obvious through an example. Coronavirus vaccines now being delivered in many countries. The question remains in many places about who should have priority to be given the vaccine first. In a purely capitalist system operating under the purest form of the Invisible Hand, it would be given to those who can afford it best. Many countries, however, have intervened to prevent this, basing the decision on who should have it first on other criteria.

Essentially, as Adam Smith himself expressed, the Invisible Hand is an ideal theoretical construct. However, be that as it may, we have all used the argument of demand and supply to justify higher compensation for something we do, or to use money to try to access something we should perhaps not have. The Coronavirus vaccine is a good case in point, as many people in the UK have tried to 'go private' to access the vaccine by paying. For the Invisible Hand to operate well, especially in a world of limited resources, an ethical element in our own actions is necessary to navigate through this moral grey zone.

The apparent power of the Invisible Hand, however, is that it takes away any need to navigate this moral grey zone. Businesses will solve our sustainability problems by themselves. The investment industry will change its focus naturally when consumers demand more goods made from recycled materials. Laws do not need to be passed for this to happen, because we will make the transition even if laws were unchanged. In this *laissez-faire* economy, only transparency and openness of access are needed. Equality and benefits accrue to all people, and individual endeavours will be rewarded fairly when those endeavours are met with appropriate demand. Profit at the point of transactions is kept in check by competition between all interested parties, and as such, the profit that is made is the measure of the service to society. This, therefore, argues for maximising profit as a moral obligation; the more profit we make, the greater the service that is offered to society.

Over the years, this argument has been used not only in businesses to motivate management and to justify practices, but it has equally been used by ourselves in arguing for our own wages. We deserve to be paid more because what we do is a social good, and equally when we are being paid more, it is because what we do brings about a greater social good.

Interventions distort this natural determination of demand and supply. In the minds of the followers of Adam Smith, interventions are necessarily evil, as they will inevitably result in inefficiencies and reduce the ability of the economy to help society. They are not needed, as the capitalist system will naturally correct itself to adjust the amount of supply and the level of demand.

Today, we produce steel, gasoline, batteries, electric power, textiles, construction materials, tyres, silicon wafers, painkillers, paper, detergents, and packaging materials all without having to know where we will use them. We grow tomatoes, corn, wheat, rice, grapes, almonds, olives, lettuces, pomelos, and cabbages in much the same way. This extends into the digital space where everything we do is profiled: shopping habits, travel routes, news interests, friends, telephone numbers, email addresses, number of times we have logged on and logged off, how long we stayed each time, how many mouse clicks. We trust the rule of demand and supply that all this will be used; if there is a surplus then prices will drop to promote new uses, and if there is a scarcity then prices will rise to prompt more production. It helps us to believe that even the tomatoes that ended up with Janne in northern Lapland had some use.

The problem with this is when resources are finite. There is no feedback to tell us that the resources have been exhausted by the sum of all of these activities, even if we each think we are operating frugally. The feedback that something is wrong may take decades or centuries to be realised. It may be that what we do is not excessive at the moment or at any moment, but that over decades, with successive unforeseeable innovations made on top of other unforeseen innovations, each incremental impact accumulates to becoming too much. This effectively is what has happened with greenhouse gases. Only after a century of use are we now recognising that we have overspent the planet's atmospheric capacity. This has happened because we have developed from factories to cars, from cars to planes, and from planes to bitcoin. Even as we realise it, it may already be too late.

No intervention by any central organisation in the past could have prevented this, because the issue is not the lack of organisation but the impossibility of foreknowledge. Even though Svante Arrhenius appreciated in 1896 that carbon dioxide will increase global temperatures and recognised that there have been periods when carbonic acid, the dissolved variant of the gas, was stored away and periods when it may be reintroduced into the atmosphere, he largely dismissed contributions from the "combustion and decay of organic bodies", essentially fossil fuels, as insignificant. The point is he could no more foresee how things turned out than we can foresee how things will turn out, despite all our claims of sustainability and regardless of how we may regulate what we do.

In truth, Adam Smith himself admitted that a free and open market is an ideal. It has, however, garnered the status of being a pillar of our economics foundation through repetition. Each time the words 'free market' are used, the concept becomes that little bit harder to refute; its authority is not derived from evidence but from inertia. Even in his own time, Smith used labour as an example to demonstrate a free market could not exist. Capital owners always had the upper hand. We argue that competition would have made fairness win out because you could not stay in business by underpaying your workers if they could demand a higher wage elsewhere. However, the reality was that capital owners colluded with each other and forced the price of labour to stay at poverty level everywhere.

Today, even though there are many more capital owners, the price of labour is still being distorted against the worker. At every level of income, we end up experiencing similar financial pressures. The fact is workers are simply trading their labour to sustain the economic cycle, with the idea of profit as a social good to justify wages being kept low. On top of this, there is also a deep but unsubstantiated belief that if workers were paid sufficiently to become comfortable, they will become lazy and productivity will suffer.

Productivity is one of these things that we keep trying to improve because it enables more profit and more growth. Productivity generally just translates into more profit, and the root of it may be traced to the scientific use of measurements by Frederick Winslow Taylor to develop his *piece-rate system*.

In 1896, he proposed the piece-rate system to reward workers according to the amount of output produced and the amount of resource used. The more a worker could produce and the faster that was produced, the more the worker would be paid. To set the rate, however, Taylor advocated measuring precisely how much time and how much material each worker needed to produce the output and then used this to categorise the skill of the workers. The better workers would be paid a premium for each unit of output, and this set a goal that others could aim for. He considered it as an improvement to the worker by giving the workers a purpose directly linked to productivity. The purpose was, of course, money. To set this in motion, the time each worker took to perform a specific task was measured precisely, as was the amount of material used. Efficiency in resources translated into productivity in output. What this also did, however, was to reduce work into activities that can be measured.

Ransom Olds was another early pioneer of transforming workplace practices to enhance output. He was a producer of motor cars in the early days of car ownership and held an impressive number of patents on every aspect of design and production. In 1901, he created the *assembly line*, with the location of the workers optimised to minimise the time lost when car parts had to be moved during the manufacturing process. With this, he was able to quintuple the number of cars he produced from his factory in a year. Henry Ford took this a significant step further and turned time itself into a component of work. In his *moving assembly line*, the car being assembled was placed on a moving conveyor belt, and the workers would add components to it as it progressed without stopping through the factory. The result was a continuous process of construction. Henry Ford was then able to have a completed Model T, his best selling car, leave the assembly line every 10 seconds of every working day. Productivity was pushed to the extreme with the costs kept low.

These improvements in efficiencies and gains in productivity have moved from the manufacturing world to the services and logistic areas in our lives. Taylor's piece-rate philosophy of paying according to productivity pretty much underlies how our wages are set; even though we may not be measured directly in terms of the number of units we produce, we are still measured against quantities of work that is expected to be done. Ransom Olds's efficiencies of space is translated into office designs, bringing closer together departments that interact with each other more frequently. Significantly, our mobile working is a reflection of the moving assembly line, where we work on the go at all times ensuring maximum throughput. When we are more efficient, however, we are not rewarded with more time off, but with more tasks to do. Our time and our space are taken over by work, and the measure of it is the pay we receive.

Today, concepts of efficiency and productivity go unchallenged. Project management tools as well as team and individual working tools all measure how long each task takes and use these measurements to create dashboards or key performance indicators to pinpoint where we have slipped and where our productivity may improve. We ourselves are often the strongest advocates for efficiency and productivity, using them to argue for our wages. We have come to accept that if it is important it needs to be measured, and often believe wrongly in the converse, if it cannot be measured it cannot be important.

There are flaws with this thinking. When we have a mathematical problem to solve, it is dubious as to whether measurements of the time taken is any indication of the quality of the solution. Even more so, something like doing less may be very important but by its very nature, it cannot be readily measured. We can only measure things that happen, we cannot measure something that does not happen even though many things are important because they do not happen. When we do less, the less is something we would struggle to benchmark. All the same, there may be a lot of benefit to doing less, but these benefits are generally not demonstrable as they are counterfactual. When we drive less, there may be fewer traffic accidents. Fewer accidents are generally easier to attribute to better driving than to driving less. It is measured in relation to the doing and not in relation to the not doing.

The concepts of measurements, efficiencies, and productivities reinforce the idea that doing as much as we can is always good. Even as we look to thinking about what we can change for sustainability, the emphasis is predominantly on doing more or doing differently, rather than doing less. Sustainable policies for example do not advocate doing less business or making less profit as the path to a more sustainable planet. Even airlines, whose business of flying has been singled out as one of the major contributors to global warming, do not mention that we should consider flying less in their sustainability policy when that may be precisely what they should at least include if they are serious about reducing their environmental impact. Similarly, no investment fund advocates that we should make fewer investments or deliberately accept lower returns as a way to reduce the pressures of financialisation. It therefore falls on us as individuals to consider our own choices.

The Invisible Hand permits us to do as much as we can without having to consider any purpose, and the ideas of efficiency and productivity help us to distance ourselves further from the need for purpose. Discussions of purpose are simply replaced by discussions of efficiency and productivity. All of this enables a system that allows our desire to grow to go unchecked, facilitated by an image of a world that has no limits to its resources.

In a different development, Toyota in the 1970s developed a production system centred on a world where continual growth was not possible. In doing so, the worker was reinstated from being an automaton to the role of an active participant. Taiichi Ohno, the in-house designer of the system, recognised the key to survival in uncertain growth environments lay in eliminating waste. Instead of the conventional manufacturing approach where you start by gathering the raw materials to produce as many cars as you can, Toyota started by asking the question in reverse. If we only need to produce one car, what would we do then? This process, therefore, starts from the actual real-world requirements, rather than from projections of what may be possible to market. It created the concept of the Kanban. This is a signboard that allows people to see all the steps in a process and how they fit together. Everyone then knows what is actually needed and when it is needed. The Kanban is now an integral part of project management processes, as well as a part of agile software development practices.

The distinction of this approach is that it is driven by what we know we need, whereas conventional mass manufacturing is driven by marketing to sell what we can produce. Here the profit is limited because there is only so much that we need, whereas for conventional mass manufacturing the profit is limitless because the scope of marketing is limitless. Minimising waste means meeting only the specific requirements we know we have and therefore the amount of resource we need is limited, whereas in conventional mass manufacturing minimising waste means producing the most number units for each unit of the resources we have, but the number of units we produce is unlimited, which means the amount of resource we will use is unlimited.

The next element to the process is something Toyota called autonomation or automation with a human touch. Referencing back to human touch is something that is characteristic of Japan. For example, their latest science and technology policy is not the familiar call for more development and commercialisation of advanced technology to achieve greater economic growth, but a call for a human-centred society that puts people and experimentation first. For a science and technology policy, it is unusual in that economics and even technology hardly gets a mention, but it focuses on the purpose of what science and technology should serve, namely, people. Autonomation recognises that machines do not need attention when they are functioning properly, and it is only when things go wrong that people are needed.

Rather than in the mass production process where workers function as automatons carrying out repetitive and menial tasks, the workers in Toyota's production system contribute at a higher level by deciding on what to do when things failed and on how best to get things back on track. This requires initiative on the part of the worker and, importantly, knowledge of the purpose of the whole process; it brings back the elements which are dismissed by the division of labour in its pursuit of blind efficiency. All this leads to an appreciation of the importance of a holistic view. The worker, as a result, is rediscovered as an active agent with responsibility for ensuring the smooth running of the whole process.

This approach is fundamentally more in tune with a world that has to live within limits. In the Toyota approach, the essence is not profit, but survival through difficult times. Eliminating waste is not about recycling or even about reusing, it is about not doing anything not needed in the first place. We are not producing to see how much we can sell; we are producing because we know how much has been requested. Our job is therefore not to increase our profits as much as possible by increasing demand, but to make the profits that we know we can achieve with the existing demand.

Toyota's development was secret and proprietary, but it was exposed unintentionally when the company maintained profits in the fallout of the 1973 oil shock. In that period, the Organization of Petroleum Exporting Countries quadrupled oil price and enforced an up to 30% cut in oil availability for Japan. In the run-up to the shock, Toyota had been concerned with how to sustain manufacturing in scenarios where an annual "economic growth rate of 6 to 10 per cent lasts at most six months to one year, with the next two or three years realizing little or no growth or even negative growth". Implicitly, this was an acknowledgement of Malthus's view that an economy always moves in fits and starts and never grows in a straight line.

Toyota moved away from inducing customers to buy vehicles indifferent to their changing economic realities and turned to understand those realities to design models that matched them. The philosophy is that it can only grow at the rate permitted by circumstances. Manufacturing efficiencies based on economies of scale work in a different way. They target a rate of growth and use economies of scale and marketing to achieve it. Our world is still very much focused in this way. Our industries make identical products for billions of people; if you want to get funded as a new sustainable startup, the basic question is how many people will purchase your solution. If the answer is anything less than a billion, then the question following would be: could it be a billion? We are then led to seeking solutions that promote more growth, and more profit.

The model of the Invisible Hand is very appealing because it is very good at promoting more growth. By breaking down a complex activity into elements, and having different people or businesses deal with them separately, means no one has to take responsibility for the impact of the totality. If we make a pin, and it is used to poison someone, we are not responsible. This allows activities to flourish, and anything can be done. If guns kill people, it is not the responsibility of the bullet maker or the gun maker. If tobacco causes cancer, it is not the responsibility of the grower, the manufacturer, the importer, the exporter, or the shopkeeper.

Each participant in the chain serves a purpose and each has profit as a reward, while the Invisible Hand shares and lightens the responsibility and the guilt of any harm caused until they become so small that they are nullified. Because everyone can claim they do not have the picture of the whole, no one is responsible. A different model like a court of law may instead hold everyone involved to be complicit and equally culpable.

In the case of complex activities, like the building of large infrastructure projects, this model of breaking everything down into independent elements needs to be reversed, and the parts need to be reaggregated back together so that the totality can be considered. Ludwig von Mises, an Austrian economist born in 1881 who emigrated to the US in 1940, developed the principles of economic calculations as a way to demonstrate how the costs and benefits of the independent elements can be aggregated back up. In doing so, the method enabled the ideas of cost-benefit analysis to develop and ultimately rationalised more activities.

By the 1920s, continued and growing inequality between the situation for labourers and capital owners spurred significant political changes. Socialist thinking and socialist economic models became established, tackling the issue of capital versus labour head-on. These models proposed intervention to force a fairer distribution to the worker, but instead of addressing the price of labour, they looked to correct the inequality in property ownership itself. Marxism, seeing the limit of capitalism as the total collapse of capitalism itself, promoted common ownership as a solution. This was realised, in a form, through the Russian Revolution.

At the time, the Austrian school of economic thinking was developed as a response to this challenge, emphasising that the best route to a sensible allocation of resources is to allow the system to correct itself. The eventual failure of communism, powerfully epitomised by the images of the fall of the Berlin Wall on 9 November 1989, is taken today as proof of the superiority of a non-interventionist and capitalist society.

Ludwig von Mises, in *A Critique of Intervention* published in 1929, argued against interventions from two standpoints. The first is an argument against public ownership. According to his thesis, in order to judge any action in a complex economy as being either good or bad, there has to be a rational means to calculate the costs and benefits of the action. Personal and political preferences cannot be relied on to decide if something is good or not. Choices must be consistent from one decision to another, and from one context to another, otherwise the distribution of resources cannot be fairly determined across the whole economy. This led to his concept of economic calculations.

Prices are necessary for such economic calculations to be possible. He argued that prices have to reflect our personal preferences and so ownership is essential. A simple example is the price of a field. To an owner, there may be a preference due to its panorama, which raises this price from a pure agricultural perspective. If the field is collectively owned, then this preference is lost. Another example is the price of a piece of the rainforest. This price will not be the same to loggers looking to clear the land as to the conservationists looking to preserve the plant and animal life. Again, if the land is publicly owned, then neither of these preferences may be expressed. The consequence is that private ownership is necessary if we are to make decisions objectively. Von Mises argued that the results of these calculations if properly performed would serve to counter-argue against prevailing political agendas.

Today, economic calculations are wrapped into cost-benefit analyses that are used by governments in major projects, such as the HS2 railway project connecting London and the north of England. They are also used by businesses for major decisions, such as the location of new data storage centres by internet companies.

Von Mises's second argument against intervention is that the origin of any inequality lies in the insufficiency of some item of necessary goods. Interventions do not create more goods. They merely shuffle the insufficient amount between different people. Because people see that the total availability has not increased, in anticipation of the reshuffling they will hoard to maintain their own advantage. Interventions will therefore lead to the opposite outcome as hoarding will reduce the openly available quantities of goods further.

Furthermore, von Mises argued in his book *Economic Calculation in the Socialist Commonwealth* that even if you were to start with a utopian state of perfection with sufficient goods, at the next increment of growth, the limits will be breached and again you will end up in a state of insufficiency. This argument follows Malthus's view that we will always run into limits and is fundamentally against the prevailing suggestions of how to face our sustainability issues.

Instead of interventions, von Mises repeated the assertions of the Invisible Hand. Private enterprises will see the demand and seek innovations either to increase the production of scarce goods or to search for alternative replacements. No one can predict how this may come about, and the Invisible Hand is credited to be better because it allows without bias all avenues of production to be explored and all possible alternatives to be considered. Intervention is simply not practical because we cannot know what the solution may be.

How do economic calculations actually work? Take an example of choosing between developing a wind farm or a nuclear power plant as the source of renewable energy. It is the same electrical energy that will be produced, serving the same community, but the costs will be different. For the wind farm, aside from the materials and the engineering costs, there will be costs to acquire the land that provides the access to the wind. This may result in a loss of revenue from agriculture. Property values within view of the wind farm may also be adversely affected. However, there will be jobs created which will benefit the local economy.

With the nuclear power plant, the engineering and construction costs can be estimated, but there will be additional costs arising from the storage of the spent nuclear materials and potentially a significant psychological impact to the local and the broader communities. Jobs are likely to be highly specialised and so may bring in more talent to the area, leading to secondary benefits. Each of these considerations can be estimated in monetary terms and aggregated into a total monetary value representing all the costs, and it may then be compared with another total monetary value representing all the benefits. The choice between the wind farm or the nuclear power plant can then be decided on based on these monetary values.

The validity of the whole framework rests on prices reflecting the values we hold important. This is more than a matter of private ownership. Because the differences in income get to be embedded into all our costs, a price of labour that properly reflects our ethical values is necessary if these calculations are to be meaningful. Without this, the tendency is such analysis will reinforce established economic biases, promoting more activities in areas that are wealthier and further extending their lead over other regions.

How should we pay the management consultant advising a major international corporation with tens of billions of revenues, and how does that compare with how we should pay the lead midwife of a group of midwives delivering 20 or so babies a day in a big city hospital? The typical day for the former is spent advising on billions of dollars' worth of costs, and what is at stake are differences in opinion. The pay here is generally a reflection of the amount of money in the industry, rationalised as the supply and demand for rare talent. The typical day for the latter is spent delicately balancing risks and medical interventions while providing emotional reassurance to strangers in life-altering moments and where mistakes mean injuries and deaths. The pay here is generally on the basis of broadly accepted costs of living, with adjustments for seniority and experience.

These pay differences impact how our various inequalities persist. For example, in the calculation of the costs versus benefits of the HS2 project, the higher wage jobs in the South East led to benefits to London being considered as more valuable than the benefits of a rail-link between cities in the north of the country where people on average earn less. This was advocated by many as a failure in the economic calculations and was eventually recognised as an error by the British government.

Incidentally, if the discrepancy in the way we pay workers in different industries is considered inappropriate, the solution is to correct the wages of the higher paid workers.

The highest paid workers are typically paid according to how much money is involved in their businesses, with the argument that higher wages are necessary to attract the calibre of people needed. This is another one of those statements which attain the status of 'truth' through repetition. Higher wages do attract more people, and some of those attracted are of high calibre. However, there are also high calibre people who do not work for the highest wages. The higher the wage, the more likely it is that more people who believe high wages are necessary are attracted. These people then reinforce their own preferences by stating high wages as universally necessary to attract talent.

The Sunday Times in the UK published the salaries of head teachers in private schools for the year 2019-2020, and the highest salary paid is £335,000. According to the Institute of Fiscal Studies using government tax data, anyone with an income of over

£160,000 is in the top 1% of earners. This means most of the headmasters are in the top 1% of earners. Is this high salary necessary to attract the talent needed to manage an academic institution? The vice-chancellor of the University of York was paid a total of £285,000 in 2020 according to the university's own remuneration report. This is £50,000 lower or 15% less than the private schools' headmaster's salary. The chancellor is credited in the report with leading the university's £1.8 billion contribution to the UK economy, managing an academic institution that has 70 departments and institutions with their associated staff and students. The chancellor further took a 20% pay cut in 2020 in light of the ramifications of the Coronavirus crisis. In this comparison, the necessity for a salary premium for the headmaster over the vice-chancellor looks dubious. The headmaster oversees the management and publicity for the school, much the same as the vice-chancellor does for the university.

The arguments for higher wages are very appealing. Evidence of others being paid highly is the best way to justify our own negotiations for higher wages. Since higher wages can only be met by more profits, we ourselves are drawn into an intervention for greater growth and consumption to achieve greater profits.

Von Mises's observation that the source of inequality lies in the limited availability of resources is not changed by us being paid more. Raising wages will simply create more pressures on goods. If we walk into a bakery with two other people looking to buy a loaf of bread and only one loaf remains, is it the best strategy to resolve the excess demand that this last loaf goes to the one who is able to pay the most for it? Paying everyone more does not alter the fact that there is only one loaf remaining; it will merely intensify the competition for that final loaf. If we are the baker, we may use the conventional argument of demand and supply to justify increasing the price until two of the three can no longer afford the loaf.

However, the argument of demand and supply is not that the price has to increase, it is only that when there is excess demand to insufficient supply, then more supply will eventually need to be created or the excess demand will eventually need to be given up. In the case of our loaf of bread, this demand and supply problem can be met by any one of the following: the client who comes in first gets the loaf; the client who looks friendliest to the baker gets the loaf; the client who failed to get the loaf the last time gets the loaf; the client who gets the loaf is randomly selected; none of the clients gets the loaf; the loaf is divided into three and is shared; or, even, two of the three clients offer the loaf to the third voluntarily.

Demand and supply do not mean that we have to resolve the situation by price bidding, but when we insist on using price as the mechanism, the result is that the more money we each have, the higher the final price will be for that loaf of bread. Since the cost of production has not changed, this only means that demand and supply settled in this way means a greater profit for the baker. So we are back to thinking that more profit is always necessary, and to accept that profits are the ultimate purpose of our activities.

The idea that demand and supply should be resolved only by pricing is very much established. Even governments do it. During the early days of the Coronavirus pandemic, the US bought personal protection equipment that had already been sold to two other European countries by paying extra. As this happens, it makes having a pool of money essential and drives up the need for escalating wages and higher and higher investment returns. It all serves to intensify our demand for growth and profits.

It is cautionary to reflect on the fact that well-intended concepts with catchy titles like 'Invisible Hand', 'productivity', 'cost-benefit analysis', and even 'social good' can all be corrupted into justifying doing whatever we want. On that note, we might be sceptical of where 'sustainability' will take us.

CHAPTER 5:

INTERVENTIONS – WE JUST CAN'T HELP OURSELVES

Governments, businesses, and policy
influencers promote growth to keep us from
hardship. When we buy into this, we make
growth a self-fulfilling prophecy and its purpose
meaningless. We can live with hardship,
but we should not live without purpose.
Stop buying into it.

The 1920s was known as the Roaring Twenties for its excesses. The period was beautifully portrayed in F. Scott Fitzgerald's book *The Great Gatsby*; during this period, radios, cars, washing machines, commercial flying, and even sliced bread became available. The mass public was given access to it all under new credit schemes, buying on instalment became commonplace, and stock market speculation was rife towards the end of the decade. All these excesses were followed by a decade of economic collapse that has come to be called The Great Depression.

In 1929, the US stock market, as represented by the Dow Jones Index, reached a peak level of 381 points in September, dropped over the course of the next three years, and bottomed in July 1932 with a staggering 90% loss. The economy, which was somewhat detached from the stock market at the time of its peak, entered into a deep depression that spread throughout the whole world. During this period, the British economist John Maynard Keynes advocated an intervention strategy for governments. This transformed growth from something that came in fits and starts into a policy objective, and this policy has continued since.

The key to this strategy is to use fiscal spending; that is, governments should spend. As people in a recession lose their jobs, they no longer have the means to keep on spending. Governments can then step in, on their behalf, to do the spending. If the Treasury coffers are empty, the government can always borrow. This money can be used to start public works, like building a new bridge. Whether the bridge is needed or not is irrelevant, as the purpose is to employ people and pay wages to them. If people have jobs, even temporarily, they can then carry on spending, and the economy will grow again.

According to this idea, governments have the power to end the business cycle. There will be no more periods of recession, and we will achieve steady and perpetual growth. This is fundamentally contrary to the idea of capitalism. Pure, idealistic capitalism is faith that people will find a way to purge the system of excesses to restart when allowed sufficient space, time and resources. We just need to be patient. Stronger proponents for capitalism have therefore argued that interventions are necessarily wrong, stopping people from taking personal responsibility for their own excesses. Once interventions start, interventions beget more interventions, and expectations grow for governments and policymakers to step in, each time with a greater commitment to protecting people from their own folly.

Keynes basically thought there was no limit to the extent governments should intervene. In his 1936 book *The General Theory of Employment, Interest Rate and Money* he wrote:

> If the Treasury were to fill old bottles with banknotes, bury them at suitable depths in disused coal mines which are then filled up to the surface with town rubbish, and leave it to private enterprise on well-tried principles of *laissez-faire* to dig the notes up again (the right to do so being obtained, of course, by tendering for leases of the note-bearing territory), there need be no more unemployment and, with the help of the repercussions, the real income of the community, and its capital wealth also, would probably become a good deal greater than it actually is. It would, indeed, be more sensible to build houses and the like; but if there are political and practical difficulties in the way of this, the above would be better than nothing.

In case there is any confusion, what he was advocating was to bury money, and to pay people to dig it back up. It is clearly a senseless activity because you could just as well have given the money freely and directly to the people. Indeed, giving free money away was what Ben Bernanke, the former chairman of the US Federal Reserve, advocated to stimulate the economy out of the 2008 Global Financial Crisis. Drop money from helicopters. In Keynes's time, however, free money was viewed as something inconceivable, so governments had to go through the charade of hiding it so that people could go through the same charade of working for it.

Keynes's suggestions were hugely transformative. Capitalist economic thinkers before him, like Malthus, Adam Smith, and von Mises, all accepted that cycles were natural, and growth periods will be interspaced with periods of recession. Chances were that recessions came about due to excessive use, and some resources had become depleted out of exuberance on our part. Interventions aim to continue the growth in spite of this, and the consequence is consumption becomes a policy tool, available for politicians and policymakers to use and abuse to continue growth. All this incidentally is with our blessing, as we have never yet voted for a political party in favour of bringing about or maintaining a recession to curb our excesses.

From this standpoint, our economic system is no longer the mechanism for the distribution of resources, but it is an engine for continued and increasing consumption.

Vance Packard, a social critic writing in the 1950s and 1960s, controversially attacked the way we had become reliant on consumption. In his books *The Hidden Persuaders* and *The Waste Makers* he highlighted the role marketing played. In the latter book, he quoted an exchange in 1958 between President Eisenhower and Robert Spivack, a journalist. That year the US and subsequently Europe and the rest of the world suffered a mild recession with growth slowing down.

The exchange, as recorded in *The American Presidency Project*, went along as follows:

> Q. Robert G. Spivack, *New York Post*: Mr President, I would like to ask you a question about what people should do to make the recession recede.
>
> THE PRESIDENT: Buy.
>
> Q. Mr Spivack: Buy what?
>
> THE PRESIDENT: Anything.
>
> Q. Mr Spivack: Well, that is just what I was going to ask you. [Laughter.] On March 26 you said at the press conference

here they should buy now, but the other day Secretary of the Treasury Anderson in New York, when he was launching the Savings Bond campaign, said they should be thrifty and put their money in bonds. [Laughter.]

THE PRESIDENT: Well, I don't say you should buy carelessly. I said to you the other day, let's be selective in our buying; let's take things we need. Look here, once America just buys the things it wants, our people, our manufacturers, will be busy making those things.

Here the President's message is clear, buy anything. Even when he is forced to explain further, his instruction is to buy anything we want.

This presidential level promotion of consumption legitimised the selling of wants as a service for the greater good. President Eisenhower described it another time in a speech given to the Advertising Council: "We sell so that they can buy our things, and we buy so they can sell. If we don't do it, our economy will be shrunken and shrivelled…" Our social duty is to consume, and marketing has become an important tool to help us do our part.

In the Coronavirus lockdowns, the same conflict appeared: do we do our utmost to eradicate the virus early, or try to navigate a neutral path of keeping consumption up while managing infection rates? Those countries which identified the issue as the prevalence of a physical virus intervened to eradicate the threat and put their faith in the ability of the economy to recover after. These were mostly Asian countries, Australia, New Zealand, and also surprisingly a number of African countries. In contrast, those who put the priority on the economy continuing unperturbed, like the UK, the US, much of Europe, and countries in South America, intervened to support the economy and ended up with a prolonged struggle.

To illustrate this point, a friend's daughter who was in Taiwan over Christmas 2020, nine months after the start of the pandemic when we were still in a strict lockdown in the UK, shared with her father pictures and videos of her and her friends celebrating and partying without any restrictions. Taiwan had chosen to deal with the virus problem right from the start, rather than to try to intervene to maintain the economy. Their economy recovered rapidly without the need for much stimulus support.

We all love to intervene; it makes us feel good to be doing something. Marketing has silently taken this to new heights so that we are now all part of an intervention for growth. Almost everything now has to have an element of advertising to it, whether it is a news article, a report we are producing, a product we are designing, or a book we are writing. These things may be sensible commercial economics, but in reality they are also our own marketing approaches to keep up consumption.

Advertising has also moved on to target our psychology; marketing is no longer about the products. Packard in his books describes a case of marketing steaks. The steaks are promoted as a convenience, and they are sold in disposable aluminium frying pans. The marketing pitch is that you can throw away the pan to save yourself the hassle of washing up; the steak does not feature in it.

In this case, as with much of the marketing in the 1950s and 1960s, the predominant narrative was about convenience. The advertising was targeting our sense of control over our time; no need for it to be wasted on chores. It subtly reinforced a sense of power. So rather than having to make the case for the steak, such as highlighting the quality of the meat, it appealed directly to our emotional drivers. These were our desire for comfort and control.

The 1920s also witnessed the beginning of *scientific advertising*. Daniel Starch was a pioneer in consumer and marketing research; after developing a successful academic career in psychology, he turned his attention to business and started a market research company. He became the first to apply scientific methods to quantify the effectiveness of the different elements employed in advertising, measuring in detail how we responded successively to the colour, image, font type, placement, and so on. He ended up being able to say how every aspect contributed to making the sale, subliminally and otherwise. Over time this has transformed the individual from an independent decision maker about what to consume, to becoming a target for incessant and subtle nudges to consume.

Ernest Dichter developed *motivational research* to tease out the subconscious and emotional roots of our decisions. He was trained as a psychoanalyst and understood that we mislead ourselves about why we do things. We argue that our actions are based on rational judgment, but he understood that emotional drivers influence us much more strongly than we allow ourselves to believe. His work allowed advertisers to target those drivers to influence our desires, and he became the marketing go-to guru for businesses.

As an example of motivational marketing, this passage regarding commercial flying given in the *Hidden Persuaders* shows the extent to which we are ourselves unaware of why we do things:

> The motivational analysts were called upon to find ways to bypass our fears, not only of products, but of situations of interest to merchandisers. One such situation that was turned over to Dr Dichter for analysis was the tearfulness of airplane passengers. American Airlines some years ago became disturbed by the fact that many of its passengers flew only when it was imperative. The airline hired a conventional research firm to find out why more people didn't fly. The answer came back that many didn't fly because they were afraid of dying. A lot of money was spent, carrying the emphasis on safety to great extremes; and according to Dr

Dichter, it didn't pay off with the increase in traffic that might be expected.

Then Dr Dichter was called in. He went into the problem in depth and even used projective tests that permitted potential travellers to imagine themselves being killed in an air crash. His investigators found that the thought in men's minds at such times was not death at all, but rather the thought of how their family would receive the news. Dr Dichter concluded that what these people feared was not death but rather embarrassment and guilty feelings, a sort of posthumous embarrassment. The husband pictured his wife saying, "The darned fool, he should have gone by train." The airline took this diagnosis seriously and began aiming its campaign more at the little woman, to persuade her that the husband would get home to her faster by flying, and to get her in the air through family flying plans. In this way, Dr Dichter explains, "The man was taken off the spot through the symbols of family approval of flying."

The rise of the internet has allowed these techniques to be deployed with scary efficiency. It creates social niches where we feel intimacy and belonging to test out our preferences in real-time and elucidate our psychological responses. All this goes back to the fundamental objective: buy. Buy what? Anything. Google, Facebook, TikTok, all the major internet platforms are not there to provide us with services; they are there to nudge our emotional responses to respond to advertising.

Sustainability is now also a huge marketing effort. Every product has a sustainable moniker attached to it, and they all offer a story of how they are contributing to making the planet better. The 2020 Coca-Cola Christmas ad is a genius of tapping into the current psyche of concern for the planet. It features a father leaving for work with a letter to Santa from his daughter. He is next shown on an offshore wind farm when he notices the letter is still in his lunch box. Realising that he has missed the last chance to send it by post, he embarks on a quest to get it to Santa. He crosses over oceans, deserts, and rainforests; he encounters whales and tree frogs, and finally, with the Northern Lights in the backdrop, he finds he is too late. Santa has already left for Christmas. In a plot twist, Santa arrives to give him a lift back home.

At the end, as a great reveal, the father sees the still undelivered letter, opens it and reads: "Dear Santa, Please bring daddy home for Christmas." As we watch the advert, it expertly triggers our emotions to think of the world as it could be, and how we as parents are willing to do everything in our power to make our children's future come true. It does not need to sell the drink, it simply brings us into the brand's family, and with that, we will naturally be inclined towards Coca-Cola in our next purchases.

Every product now aims to do likewise, using the planet to induce us into forgetting that we are consuming. In the 1920s the movement was women's rights and the Coca-Cola posters then depicted women enjoying a coke by themselves, while they were playing tennis, or even as an aviator. These were bold images for the time. The sort of independence portrayed was not only inspirational, but it was also highly controversial and widely frowned upon. However, the image of a woman being in charge of herself and of her future was reaching into a new market of consumers, namely those who could choose for themselves. This sort of advertising, by tapping into the issues we consider important, is very effective because it makes us feel better about ourselves.

Sustainable investing and sustainable growth are doing the same; few of those who subscribe to them actually understand how sustainability will be achieved. We follow because they resonate with our thinking, and therefore we are willing to be nudged to participate in the consumption offerings.

In the post-Second World War years, food, diseases, and shelter issues in developed countries had improved to such an extent that Barbara Castle, the chairman of the 1959 Labour Party Conference in the UK, had to admit, "The poverty and unemployment which we came into existence to fight have been largely conquered." In accordance with Maslow's hierarchy of needs, our natural wants then moved on to psychological ones. This was perfectly timed for the use of psychology in marketing. In *The Hidden Persuaders*, Packard listed eight psychological factors that marketers targeted and which are still being targeted. These are *emotional security, reassurance of worth, ego-gratification, creative outlets, love objects, sense of power, sense of root*, and *immortality*. They are the buttons advertisers push to stimulate us to consume.

How it actually works is very subtle, and is by now so ingrained into our lives that we reinforce it in each other without thinking. We have all become a part of advertising, and that is its great power. We do not even notice it when we are pushing each other, as agents of advertising, into promoting a particular pattern of growth and consumption.

For example, the PWC report on asset management, *Asset Management 2020: A Brave New World*, creates a fictional character, Wei. This is used to represent the typical user of asset management; she is Chinese because China is the next growth market for the industry. In keeping with the way our journalism now largely works, everything is arranged around anecdotes to give it a more human feel. The cold, emotionless presentation of data and evidence is replaced by storytelling, engendering a more emotional engagement.

Wei is a professional; she has a son and an ambition to educate him abroad. The story starts with her commute from the suburb of Beijing. As she is heading into her office, she receives a message from an internet dating service. The narrative is of a young woman who is competent in her work, and she hopes for a promising future for her son and fulfilment for herself. The writers of the report, with or without intending it as validation of a way of life, craft her profile to repeat and reinforce the aspirations that we are constantly being suggested. These include things like an implied Ivy League college education, a successful career, a meaningful personal relationship, and so on. In this way, the writers unconsciously become agents of marketing, promoting particular hopes and desires, and subtly enabling the industry to shape our ambitions.

The report goes on to ask, "Will Wei achieve her dream of building a portfolio that will enable her son to study abroad?" These words play on our sense of responsibility for our loved ones and on our need for emotional security about their future. They are pushing on those buttons we mentioned earlier and equally build to offering a sense of worth and purpose for the investment professional. The passage finishes with "millions like her around the world depend on the asset management industry to help them fulfil their ambitions". Who would not want to do that? The message is investing is a good profession to be involved in. These statements are placed so the reader can take them up as a mantra to repeat for the investment industry, legitimising through each repetition the pursuit of high returns.

So, by now we have all come to be part of the economic system that focuses on maintaining and continuing growth, and we are now the marketers for it. We post pictures and videos on our social media of things we like, intentionally or inadvertently becoming part of their promotion. The rise of social media influencers is yet another step in this progression. In a reversal of roles, manufacturing and service industries are no longer there to meet our actual needs, but we – that is you, me, and each and every one of us – promote and create ever-increasing demands to keep those businesses going.

The next step of intervention to ensure that growth continues comes in the form of printing money directly. Government interventions on demand can only go so far because governments need tax revenue to support their spending, and in democratic countries, political parties implementing high taxation typically do not get re-elected. Further, as obvious in the current Coronavirus situation, it is not possible to tax when there is no income. Central banks are lured into printing money for us. The money printed, however, does not come to us directly, we still have to work for it. It is not there to support us; it is there to promote more activities. So, the money goes towards lowering the hurdles needed for sensible investments. For the planet, this means allowing resources to be exploited for free.

In the period leading into the 2008 Global Financial Crisis and since, central bankers who control the amount of money and credit available in the economy have stepped in to be the torchbearers to promote growth. Our economic system no longer operates with a gold standard where the money would be fixed by the physical amount of gold held by central banks. The amount of money available is limited only by rules that can change to make money more or less available. The way it works is as follows:

The central bank is the institution managing the total amount of money available in the country. It sets rules to govern commercial banks. Commercial banks are the banks with which individuals and businesses have accounts. These banks are required to deposit a portion of the money we put in them with the central bank. The central bank is the safest place for our money, and it offers interest to the commercial banks on any money deposited. By raising the level of the interests offered, the central bank attracts more money to be deposited with it and therefore takes money out of the general economy. Alternatively, by lowering the interest rate, it disincentivises the commercial banks from keeping money with it, and pushes the commercial banks to lend out more money to people and businesses.

The amounts involved are huge; measured in aggregate across all commercial banks it comes to trillions of dollars, so the amount of interest paid, even for one single day, is substantial. For example, a bank like JP Morgan may have $1.5 trillion dollars entrusted to it in its deposits. If it keeps 10% of it for safety, and if the central bank's interest rates were, say 5% – something that has not been seen for a very long time – then for each night JP Morgan will earn $20 million.

After the Global Financial Crisis, a concerted effort was made by the world's major central banks to increase lending to businesses. This was done by lowering their official interest rate which resulted in less incentive for the commercial banks to keep money with the central bank; the interest rate was then reduced multiple times until it eventually reached zero. At this point, the commercial banks have no incentive to keep any money on deposit with the central bank. They therefore lowered the interest rates businesses and people would have to pay to borrow. This meant that business ideas could be funded at very low costs.

When central bank interest rates were lowered to zero, economists began to speculate what more could be done to get the economy back on track. People and businesses were still not borrowing enough. The problem was that we needed to change away from property speculation, and that needed time and patience to discover other opportunities more than it needed money.

The policy focus, however, was to push for growth. On 11 June 2014, the European Central Bank (ECB) moved its official interest rate to negative levels. Commercial banks were now punished if they left money with the central bank; every night money was left deposited there would cost the commercial banks a penalty. This also applied to any pension funds, large corporations, or wealthy individuals with a lot of savings in banks.

The implications were extreme and devastating. In a world where you are being punished for taking the time and being prudent, reckless ventures begin to look attractive. The stimulus motivation worked. This initially prompted investments and lending to high-quality companies, but these opportunities soon became exhausted. Then, prices for residential properties quickly recovered and surpassed the levels which led to the Global Financial Crisis, and as recognised opportunities began to dry up, any activity with a sellable story was invested in. It was like investing to dig up Keynes's 'old bottles' except this time knowing that the bottles had no money in them.

With investors now being punished for keeping money in the safest place possible, asset bubbles began to form everywhere. Bitcoin, classic cars, art − even the third edition of a banana duct-taped to the wall sold for $120,000 − everything became legitimate investments. The more the central banks tried to reflate the economy by pumping money, the more activities whose only motive is profit flourished. Those who could get on to this asset bubble became rich, but in reality, everyone felt they were getting poorer.

The situation with negative rates continued for the best part of a decade. In Denmark, it became possible to take out a 10-year mortgage with negative interest rates; each month, what is owed is automatically reduced by the 'generosity' of the central bank. It eventually meant for some people it became possible to be paid to borrow money. Social inequalities grew and rampant exploitation of physical resources ensued, enabled by free money from central banks.

The bike-share business is an example of this exploitation. It became very popular on the back of the idea of car sharing. The business works in cities where distances are small, and population density is high. Through the combination of GPS tracking and mobile apps, people can register and pick up a bicycle from the roadside and use it for a journey. To start the venture, a large number of bicycles is needed, to be placed liberally everywhere so that they are readily available on the roads.

Successive competing entrants to this market flooded the streets with bicycles in cities, especially in China where the population is very high, and later in other major cities around the world. The bicycles were painted in bright colours and served as advertising. The more bicycles there were, the more they served to bring attention to the business. The consequence was countless bicycle graveyards, each containing tens of thousands of discarded bikes representing wasted materials and energy. It was made possible because negative interest rates allowed investors to borrow and earn interest from borrowing, as investing in highly speculative ventures was still better than keeping it in banks to face certain loss.

Central banks started to become significant agents for providing stimuli in the Reagan-Thatcher era. During this period, politics moved towards smaller governments, returning the responsibility for social welfare back to individuals and promoting the idea of trickle-down prosperity, where successful individuals who got rich would spend and create opportunities for others to follow. As this became an integral part of the right-wing political manifesto, governments pulled back from direct subsidies, and central banks took up a greater role in interventions to stimulate the economy.

Financial markets started to look to central bank policies more closely. Alan Greenspan, appointed by President Reagan in 1987 as the chairman of the US's Federal Reserve, played a central part in shaping the way central bankers have come to consider this role.

Greenspan was a member of Ayn Rand's inner circle. Originally named Alisa Zinovyevna Rosenbaum, Rand was born in 1905 in Russia and lived through the revolution as a child. She saw her family's business confiscated, and later, before going to America, she was purged from Petrograd State University for being a bourgeois student. In America, she changed her name and became a very vocal voice against any form of collectivism, claiming everything except the most extreme form of individualism as evil.

The only moral path for society to her, as published in 1944 as *The Only Path to Tomorrow*, lay in considering man as "an independent entity with an inalienable right to the pursuit of his own happiness in a society where men deal with one another as equals".

This promotion of the pursuit of our own happiness as a moral imperative became a form of personal intervention to promote growth. We already have economic theories promoting profits as a social good, and governments using consumption as policy tools to enforce growth. Advertising is already reaching into our individual psyches to help us justify our consumption habits. Now, with individualism advocating there is a moral basis for pursuing whatever we want, any remaining ethical considerations that there may be to hold back on our consumption are removed. Rand's manifesto may assert that men should deal with each other as equals, but in reality, we know too well, and expressed by George Orwell in *Animal Farm*, "Some animals are more equal than others." With individualism, we now all have the right and can demand to be treated as the 'more equal' animal.

Today Ayn Rand's philosophy still carries tremendous appeal. The fictional hero, Howard Roark, in her novel *The Fountainhead* is an architect who owes nothing to others. He is the torchbearer of individualism, where he claims that by his own brilliance he creates the buildings which benefit others. He is godlike, and others are mortals who are too lowly to provide any benefit to him in return. He is the 'active man' who makes things possible. To Ayn Rand, the active man is responsible for all of our progress, the rest are simply 'passive men' who contribute nothing to our development. Therefore, the world owes the active man and his individualism in a way that should be even beyond the restraints of any law. Any attempt to hold him accountable for his action is to side with collectivism, the ultimate evil for Ayn Rand, which is perhaps understandable given her background.

The active man is clearly the more equal animal, and in the novel, he destroys the building he designed, claiming the full and essential right to the physical materials and human labour used in its construction simply because it pleases him to destroy it. He claims the right to lay waste all the resources that others have contributed and make them unavailable for anyone else. In a reversal of Keynes's idea of intervention, which was to promote growth for the benefit of everyone, Howard Roark's intervention is an expression of our right to destroy the world for our own pleasure. Unfettered, self-serving individualism, in the end, becomes an expression of the crab mentality: if I can't have it, then neither can you.

However, the idea that one group is more deserving than another is very appealing. Many politicians have used Rand's arguments to rationalise their claim to power. The language of Donald Trump is not much different from that of Howard Roark. It is a world where we have the right to come first. Our purpose for interventions is to put ourselves first.

Greenspan implicitly rationalised that it is acceptable for growth to come at the expense of others. At a dinner speech in 1996 which is now infamously known as the 'irrational exuberance' speech, he rhetorically asked, "How do we know when irrational exuberance has unduly escalated asset values?" At the time, stock market prices were at their historical highest and there were concerns that these were driven by exuberance rather than by rational expectations of the future. Many felt that the high prices were damaging to society. In answering, he justified inaction to prevent asset bubbles from building: "We as central bankers need not be concerned if a collapsing financial asset bubble does not threaten to impair the real economy." This set a policy of non-intervention, but only in the sense of Ayn Rand's individualism.

When asset bubbles form, those who are the active men take part to create the larger than life exuberances and should not be prevented from their efforts. In line with the ideas of trickle-down prosperity, these efforts may lead to benefits for passive men. Intervening to prevent excesses would therefore be wrong as it would hinder our individualistic right and prevent the possibility of benefits accruing for society.

Non-intervention thus becomes also an intervention for growth.

The problem with promoting growth ultimately comes back to whether there are boundaries to our planetary and societal resources or not. Fundamentally, the desire is to enforce a steady and perpetual growth according to our own dictates. If resources are finite, then this desire will ultimately create a sustainability problem.

Q&A

Q: Practically, for me as an individual, I don't want to suffer. The comments are that it will cost us more if our environmental problems aren't sorted now. So, if I don't want to pay the economic penalties, what can I do to make it better? For me, and for everyone?

A: We will have to pay economic penalties. When we make money by doing something bad, we will lose the money when we stop doing the bad thing. So it is not about avoiding economic penalties but about making our lives better.

We make things better for others and for ourselves by having a sense of purpose that helps us accept sacrifices.

The answer, therefore, lies in ethics. We have to ask, what are we living for? This is a question for each of us. If we work as an accountant, do we get satisfaction from helping people's finances, or is it just an activity to give us a wage? If we only work for a wage, then where do we get satisfaction for living from?

Knowing from where we get genuine satisfaction helps us to know where we can accept sacrifices.

In a world running out of resources, we are all connected. What others sacrifice becomes available for us, and what we sacrifice becomes available for them, so we need to be other-serving if we are to live with a purpose.

CHAPTER 6:

THE CALIFORNIA GOLD RUSH

When money is too readily available, everything becomes expensive, and it is fundamentally destructive. Be careful what you wish for.

We stumbled on to the story of the California Gold Rush in our research for this book. I was reading aloud about the details of irrigation in vineyards in California when Richard, who is knowledgeable in these matters and appalled by the idea, exclaimed, "Vines should never be irrigated."

Digging further into the issues brought up the problems associated with water usage, water rights, water toxicity, and the conflicts between people and agriculture in the state. It was not long before references to the Gold Rush started popping up. So much of today's problems with water in California, in one way or another, are the relics of an event over 170 years ago.

As we researched further into the details of what happened during the Gold Rush, we were surprised at how the events of the period resonated with us as a warning of what we are facing now. It was a world where the promises of riches drove activities insane and pulled everyone from all around the world into a frenzied mania. However, money did not equate to its promises. Money was extracted freely from the ground as gold, but true wealth did not materialise. In a similar way, financial returns in investments are easily obtained when the whole world believes in them, but in no way do the returns equate to what we hope they will provide for us in our lives.

We also felt moved by a deeper aspect of the Gold Rush. First-hand accounts of two women at different points in time during that period and living under different circumstances both concluded that, despite their hardships, uncertainties, failures, and disappointments, they managed a life well-lived. We felt this was achieved not because of any certainties they were able to bring to their lives, but from an acceptance that there were no certainties. It brought into our own thinking the differences between relying on the promise of certainty that money makes, and accepting the likely reality of an uncertain future. It made us think of what it is that we should be living for.

And so, to the Gold Rush.

John Sutter, who owned the land on which gold was first discovered, and James Marshall, who made the discovery, both gave first-hand accounts of the events in *Hutchings' California Magazine* in 1857. Sutter left his family and debts behind in Switzerland, and arriving in Fort Vancouver in Portland in 1838, he had the ambition to build a settlement for Swiss immigrants. As a demonstration of the difficulties and hazards facing overland travel at that time, instead of a journey across the country, he opted for a 10,000 kilometre sea voyage; he sailed from Portland to Honolulu, Honolulu to Alaska, before arriving finally at Yerba Buena which would later become San Francisco.

California was then not yet part of the United States, and there were still territorial disputes with Spanish Mexico as well as conflicts with the native population. The idea of a settlement providing a buffer helped to convince the governor to grant Sutter 50,000 acres for his New Helvetia. The land came with a requirement that the natural rights of the local Indians must be preserved.

James Marshall was contracted to help Sutter build a sawmill. At the time, apart from the indigenous population, there were only a few hundred people settled in California, so if you needed something you had to build it yourself. Sutter wanted a settlement that was intended to be constructed around farming and needed a flour mill. For that, he needed timber, and to make that possible, he needed a sawmill. He partnered with James Marshall and located a forested site in Coloma with good access to water to provide power.

By the time Sutter and Marshall wrote their articles, the Gold Rush was coming towards the end and Sutter was ruined. He had lost everything to land grabbers and squatters who outright stole his land and his properties. The combination of the transitional state of California at the time and the fact that what was done during the Gold Rush was new and did not meet with any clear precedents meant that his attempts at legal resolution were consistently foiled. It is a sombre reflection, which we can witness today, that economic activities which disrupt the *status quo* are often less innovative than they are claimed, but do so simply by exploiting gaps in the law.

James Marshall discovered gold between 18 and 20 January 1848, during a routine inspection of the watermill. The work was near completion, and the news was initially kept secret to allow the work on the mill to finish. It eventually leaked out, not least by Sutter himself when he was called to confirm the authenticity of gold pieces one of his workers used to pay for brandy. The *Californian*, a San Franciscan weekly paper of the time, first mentioned John Sutter and his gold in its 15 March edition. By May, the strike was well known locally and had attracted so many people to prospecting that Sutter commented, on a visit to San Francisco that month, that "only five men were left to take care of the women and children".

This was an echo of Malthus's critique of how high wages deplete labour from essential services.

People on the east coast of America, however, were more reluctant to believe in the news of the discovery. Rumours circulated that it was a ruse on Sutter's part to attract people to his settlement. It was only after President Polk mentioned it in his December 1848 *Message to Congress on the State of the Union* address that the issue of gold discovery in California was settled. In the speech, the president authorised a mint to be established in California. Even the government was going to be in on it.

California's population is now about 40 million. At the time when Sutter arrived, aside from Native Americans, there were maybe a few hundred people spread over an area about twice that of the UK. Sutter was lucky to have had 238 delisted members of the Mormon Battalion, led by Samuel Brannan, travelling through to help him with building his settlement. The Mormons had been persecuted in the Eastern States as their religious practices were disapproved of. The Governor of Missouri, Lilburn Boggs, went so far as to issue in 1838 an order that all Mormons "must be treated as enemies and must be exterminated or driven from the state", an order only rescinded in 1976.

The religious group needed funds to finance an exodus to the West for their survival. Their leader, Brigham Young, made a deal with the US Army to enlist 500 men and form a Mormon Battalion to help fight border conflicts as a way to re-establish goodwill. The soldiers' pay enabled their migration and over the course of a year, the battalion circumscribed the United States, traversing through Kansas, New Mexico, Arizona, California, on to Nevada, Idaho, Wyoming, Nebraska, and eventually via Colorado to settle with the main Mormon community near Salt Lake in Utah. For Sutter, the arrival of the Mormons provided him with the workforce he needed; it also meant they were the first to be on-site for the gold discovery which provided them with the capital to establish their eventual community.

Samuel Brannan was one of the first outsiders to know of the gold discovery, being a partner to the man who had sold the brandy to Sutter's worker. As an indication of the profiteering, racketeering and hoarding practices that became commonplace, Brannan immediately started to stockpile supplies and laid claim to Mormon Island where the Mormons under his leadership were staying and demanded a 30% finder's fee for any gold they discovered.

The story of the California Gold Rush is also a story of how money rapidly led to inflation, with the result that even when money was made, the cost of living had already outstripped its purchasing power. James Narron, senior vice-president of the Federal Reserve Bank of San Francisco, stated that at one point it would have been cheaper to ship dirty clothes to Hawaii than to have them laundered locally. We see some things similar today in the rise in house prices over the past decade, in the level of the stock market, and worryingly, in the returns on investments. As people clamber over each other in a desire to be a part of it, whether it is homeownership, savings investments, or sustainability transformation, the first result is inflation. As things become expensive and more people get to be involved, fear and scarcity develop to enable pure profit motives to take over.

The price of inflation is recounted in a collection of letters written by a couple who ventured to California in 1848, early in the Gold Rush. The letters are published together under the title *Apron Full of Gold*. The couple left Maine, leaving behind unaffordable debts and three children to travel by sea southwards along the east coast of America, crossing the continent through Panama to continue northwards by sea again to San Francisco. They made this journey more than once, as they travelled back to their children before returning again.

The letter from Mary Jane Megquier, written when she finally arrives for the first time in California, sums up both the expectation of free money and the reality of inflation:

> We have been here three days and have had nothing to eat but beef, pickled fish and poor flour bread. What think of that? [sic] If I could only get a house to live in I should make money but one boarding house rents for eighty thousand dollars a year, rent and labour is the reason board is so high, money is plenty as dirt if you have any means of getting hold of it, but we have not been here long enough to tell whether we can make anything or not, but if your Father can get practice there will be no doubt but we can get money enough in a year or two to come home, there is seven millions of gold dust in this little place besides thousands of coined money, some that came on in the boat with us have made a fortune in speculations while others have been ruined.

> Money is everywhere and plenty as dirt, and everything is expensive; in three days it is possible to be completely ruined or to have made a fortune.

To put this in context, a quick check on *Apartments.com* today shows the rent for a four-bed townhouse in the Panhandle district of central San Francisco is about $50,000 a year today. The cost of the boarding house was $80,000 a year for Mary Jane, more than 170 years ago at the time of the Gold Rush.

As for the couple, at the time, their letters tell that they did make some money. Mary Jane writes soon after, "We have made more money now than we could make in two years at home", and in another letter, "We have made more money since we have been here than we should make in Winthrop in twenty years." However, the difference between having a large nominal sum of money and what you can do with it is emphasised in a letter by the husband when he writes, "Business is getting better although money is very tight… money is bringing fifteen per cent per month."

Again, to put this in context, 15% a month means you will be paying almost $27 in a year's time for a meal that costs you only $5 today.

On many occasions, Mary Jane talks of the streets becoming impassable because of mud a foot deep, and in a letter in 1852, when things had settled down, she writes that mud was still "four inches deep all over the house when the street was having a sewer laid." The livelihoods away from gold mining were not easy either. She tells of droughts, fires and floods which regularly destroyed lives:

> You have no idea the distress in this country now, a fire in Sacramento City, then a flood, has bankrupted many, & has deprived the farmers of putting in their wheat crops early, which may prove an entire failure, so you perceive this country depends entirely upon circumstances, if favourable all right, if not, the reverse.

All this emphasised the disconnect between the ready availability of money and the hardships of living.

While Mary Jane stayed mainly in San Francisco, the story of life in a mining community was told in the *Shirley Letters*. These were written by Louise Amelia Knapp Smith Clappe, a school friend of Emily Dickinson. She wrote her letters to her sister Molly as 'Dame Shirley'.

Louise Clappe travelled with her husband from Massachusetts to California to take advantage of the Gold Rush and the opportunities it represented. They arrived with her husband having fallen sick during the journey. This was a common occurrence given the hardships travelling entailed at the time. From her letters, she writes that the air of the city is too polluted for his weakened condition, which says a lot about the state of the city, and upon recommendation, they move to a mining settlement called Rich Bar to take advantage of cleaner air, and because, according to a friend, "there were a thousand people there already, and but one physician". Her husband is a qualified doctor. However, by the time they arrive at the settlement, "there were twenty-nine who had chosen this place for the express purpose of practicing their profession."

This was an example of the fear of missing out, an expression used to describe behaviour that can often lead to catastrophic outcomes, especially in finance. When enough people are expecting and promised great things, especially when it is financial returns and money, others begin to fear being left behind. Everyone then looks for ways to participate and it rapidly becomes an overwhelming and self-justifying movement.

In both Mary Jane and Louise Clappe's letters, people with skills and trades like mechanics, as well as entertainers, and, of course, swindlers and fraudsters all joined the Gold Rush, and physicians swarmed to the mining settlements hoping to share in the profits, only to find too many others exactly like them.

Louise Clappe keenly observes what life is like living in the settlements in her letters. Rich Bar has a hotel called the Empire, and it alone has glass in its windows. Other good-quality cabins in her descriptions have no need for glass as they have no windows, and are lit through space where eventually there may be a door. Rich Bar is a part of the river morphology, and the settlement develops there purely for the purpose of gold prospecting; life is ever at risk.

From her letters, the miners often believe that the more substantial veins are to be found in the bed-rock, and they sink deep shafts in the hope of striking one. The place is littered with these shafts in all directions, all open and unprotected. In her fourth letter, Louise Clappe recounts how a young miner simply fell to his death in one. Death, mutilations, life-threatening sickness are never far away. The quiet periods are when death is not coming from mining, but death happens all the same. She writes:

> It is extremely healthy here. With the exception of two or three men who were drowned when the river was so high, I have not heard of a death for months.

She devotes one letter to describe the death of Mrs B. Women were extremely rare in the Gold Rush. In the letter, she explains how Mrs B is one of only four women among the thousands of men, so her death from peritonitis, an infection that she contracted only four days before she dies, is devastating. In one of her other letters, she talks of speaking with the finder of Rich Bar who has not spoken with a woman for two years. The women who are there are tough, and she writes of another of how "she walked to this place, and packed fifty pounds of flour on her back down that awful hill, the snow being five feet deep at the time".

Life is an incessant occupation with mining. She describes how the landscape is beautiful, but the noise is unbearable. The fluming machines work incessantly, keeping up "the most dismal moaning and shrieking all the livelong night, painfully suggestive of a suffering child". Noises come also from the bowling-alley, which "never leaves off for ten consecutive minutes at any time during the entire twenty-four hours" and on Sundays "it never leaves off for one minute". There is never any peace, only what she calls "sleep-murderers".

Louise Clappe's time living in a mining camp came to an abrupt end when Indian Bar, a site she moved to with her husband to build a log cabin as a permanent home, was abandoned. In a place where only a few months earlier hundreds of people arrived, and saloons sprung up in every direction, and fluming operations rapidly progressed, she writes, "Not twenty men remaining on Indian Bar, although two months ago you could count them up by hundreds." She also writes of the collapse of the settlement:

> Of course the whole world (our world) was, to use a phrase much in vogue here, 'dead broke'. The shopkeepers, restaurants, and gambling houses, with an amiable confidingness peculiar to such people, had trusted the miners to that degree that they themselves were in the same moneyless condition. Such a batch of woeful faces was never seen before, not the least elongated of which was F's [her husband], to whom nearly all the companies owed large sums.

It may seem peculiar to read that even gambling houses would have trusted the miners to such an extent that they too become dead broke. In reality, with prices escalating at such a phenomenal pace, there was no choice. Everyone was caught in sequences of transactions and deals which left them fully committed to keeping the miners working. It was always a case of doubling down to continue for longer in the hope of winning later, as stopping at any point meant bankruptcy. While a gold strike might have allowed them to break even, it would have been unlikely to have made many of them rich. Stopping would have meant certain destitution.

When we read the accounts and thought about the lives of the people and their need despite all the money to keep pushing at that time, our frenzied push for growth in the name of sustainability seems similar. Are we not simply doubling down on the same strategy to grow our way out of the problems?

The activities of the Gold Rush were incredibly wasteful.

Thomas Megquier, Mary Jane's husband, notes in one of his letters that "there must be from three to five millions of money, destroyed by the loss of goods that cannot be stored the coming winter." As he explains, shop owners hoard to raise prices, and the miners hold off from purchasing in a game of brinksmanship that ends in starvation and the loss of goods.

This seems vengeful now, but again, in reality, at the time, both sides had costs to cover. The expectation of more money in the future made everybody knowingly pay too much. In the end, investments, whether they were in perishable goods, mining equipment, time, or even simply hard labour never delivered enough.

We think that we are at serious risk of making the same bet and similarly creating inflation in our investments for a sustainability transformation. As we have mentioned before, sustainability promises cannot be guaranteed. We simply do too much, but like the shopkeepers, restaurants and gambling houses, stopping is not an option. There is a genuine cost to stopping, and against that, we can cling to a promise of a better future by continuing. So we accept the businesses' reassurances that with their sustainability policies, the world will be transformed. In reality, our businesses can no more promise sustainability to us than the miners could promise gold to the shopkeepers. In spite of suspecting this, we pay higher and higher prices to support these businesses in their claims.

The 1840s and 1850s was a time of political unrest and famine around the world. In southern China, famine and severe economic depression followed the Unequal Treaties and the Opium War; 20 million lives were lost in the Taiping Rebellion. In Europe, 1848 started with the overthrowing of the French King Louis-Philippe, and a series of populist revolutions spread across 50 countries; the period became known as the Springtime of the People and created havoc and misery for many. Famines in Europe were common during these years, including the Irish Potato Famine which cost millions of lives. These events provided a big impetus to emigration.

Against this backdrop, 300,000 people from everywhere in the world converged on California, and this influx ran up against the Native American population. The travellers brought along new diseases which decimated the natives. Further, as resources became scarce, competition led to battles for survival. In the Governor's message to the Senate and Assembly, at the Second Session of the California Legislature in 1851, he unapologetically acknowledged, "We have suddenly spread ourselves over the country in every direction, and appropriated whatever portion of it we pleased to ourselves, without their consent, and without compensation", and finished by saying "that a war of extermination will continue to be waged between the races until the Indian race becomes extinct must be expected."

Dame Shirley, writing at the time, recounts how the persecution of Spanish miners grew as the gold yield decreased and Mad Max-style vigilantism took over.

As gold mining became less and less profitable, California imposed a miner's tax on foreigners. The repercussion of institutional discrimination raged on; the federal *Chinese Exclusion Act* was later passed in 1882 and banned Chinese from entering America for 10 years. Racial discrimination became international, with Australia imposing a heavy tax on entry as well as a poll tax for residency on the Chinese during Australia's own gold rush.

Problems created by our sustainability transition such as with the lithium mining we talked about earlier are not dissimilar to what was happening at the time. As we rush into a transition, we risk making resources scarcer and creating the backdrop for power grabs justified on the basis of a greater good. Social injustices are prone to follow as profiteering takes precedence.

The amount of gold extracted was phenomenal. Gold became money. Gold dust was used, as stated in advertisements in the *Californian*, as everyday payments. Gold production peaked in 1852, and on average 76 tonnes were extracted each year, much of it in the first year or so after the discovery. To put 76 tonnes of gold in context, the metal is so dense that it would fit in the boot of a large family car with the rear seats removed. As a comparison, the cumulative gold production in the previous 55 years in the US was, in total, only 37 tonnes, half the amount of a single year's average during the Gold Rush. The effect of this injection of money is like giving everyone in the space of three months their entire lifetime earnings. With all that money suddenly available, the indigenous Native Americans were massacred; the land was poisoned; racism was institutionalised; most people suffered and prices went out of control; hoarding became the norm.

What saved California and transformed it from the mania of the Gold Rush into prosperity today was the vast and untapped resources of the country. The 1850s happened when much of the planet was still available to be exploited. Agriculture was undeveloped in California and the trans-American railroad did not yet exist. Nicaragua and Panama were waiting for the 20,000 travellers each year who went between the East Coast and the West Coast to provide them with opportunities. There was still plenty of room for global trade to expand. These all provided room for developments to mend the damages that were done.

If we believe sustainability is a genuine issue, this solution is not available for us. We now start with a planet where the boundaries are much nearer. Globalisation has reached a level where further trade expansion is an issue, and travel is now widely seen as highly damaging. The limits of the planet are much more pronounced than they ever were in the 1850s, and the scope to grow and rely on technology as a way out of our predicament is much more restricted.

When we look back to the Gold Rush, we also see the problems that rapid uptakes of new technologies can create. Hydraulic extraction, which literally used water under huge pressures to break away sides of mountains, left scars that are still visible today. Water ditches, which provided extensive means to divert water for mining, created the *prior approbation* right of ownership; that is, first come first served regardless of any other considerations. This has led to the deprivation of water and conflicts over waters rights that have lasted to today. Mercury was introduced as a technology to facilitate the separation of gold from the mud and the rocks. As mercury is quite toxic, it has left California with a problematic legacy. The Water Education Foundation, a non-profit organisation, reported that an estimated 10% of the state's landmass would have to be dredged if it were to be decontaminated.

All these issues aside, the people and the accounts from Mary Jane Megquier and Dame Shirley give us hope. In the end, Mary Jane Megquier returned to Maine to be close to her children, but before leaving, she writes:

> Never in my life did I live as free as now, I have a fine circle of friends, sew for Mrs Calkins to pay my board, I rent the building for a trifle enough to find me in what I must have.

In the same letter, in case we feel the image is an idyllic living, she gives a description of the then state of affairs in San Francisco:

> Many can neither eat, nor sleep, they say the law and order people will plunder and burn the city, and there is no knowing what will become of the women, and children, I assure you it looks very like war.

Dame Shirley too ultimately returned to the East Coast after working as a teacher for many years in San Francisco. Her stay at the mining camp, as we have said, was cut short by the collapse of the town as the gold ran out.

In spite of that, or, maybe because of it, she expresses in her final letter before she left:

> My heart is heavy at the thought of departing forever from this place. I like this wild and barbarous life. I leave it with regret... I took kindly to this existence, which to you seems so sordid and mean. Here, at least, I have been contented.

The words 'free' and 'contented' stand out in these statements. Neither had made their fortune in the way they had hoped. Both were still living with much hardship. What was it that gave them a sense of purpose in that very uncertain world? This may be a better thing for us to understand and possibly to aim for than for the apparent security of financial wealth or a blind belief in the promises of sustainability. The Gold Rush was a promised dream of a prosperous future for everyone involved, but ultimately not attained.

CHAPTER 7:

THE GFC – A SHORT LESSON IN REFLEXIVITY

Having good intentions does not equate to achieving good outcomes.

The Global Financial Crisis happened because we all wanted better for ourselves.

On 7 February 2007, the UK-based international bank HSBC issued a trading update. These are usually issued when information significant to a company's business has come to light and needs to be told promptly to all its shareholders. Typically, these have strong implications on the value of the company and the price at which its shares are trading. The statement said:

> The impact of slowing house price growth is being reflected in accelerated delinquency trends across the US sub-prime mortgage market, particularly in the more recent loans, as the absence of equity appreciation is reducing refinancing options.
>
> We now expect that the impact of increased provisioning in this area will be the major factor in bringing the aggregate

of loan impairment charges and other credit risk provisions to be reflected in the accounts of the Group for the year ended 31 December 2006 above consensus estimates* by some 20 per cent.

Basically, this update was saying that people were failing to make their mortgage payments, and as house prices were no longer going up, they were also unable to refinance their debt. As a result, the bank would lose a lot of money.

Back in 2003, HSBC bought a US company called Household International. This company was focused on providing loans to people who did not have perfect credit records. At the time when Household International was being bought, it had the impressive ability to process a loan application in under two seconds. It had to slow this down in practice so that customers could feel their applications had received proper attention. HSBC made the purchase to participate in the then-booming residential property market in the US.

The trading update was a warning sign of the global catastrophe that was to follow. People who had taken out mortgages in the decade before were beginning to find themselves in trouble. Many of those who took out mortgages closer to 2007 were offered very favourable teaser interest rates for the first year or two, which would promptly increase to unaffordable levels after. The low interest rates in the initial period allowed people to get on to the housing ladder. At the time, house prices were increasing year on year, and it was confidently felt by all parties that it would be possible either to sell the house for a profit or to get a new mortgage based on a higher house price before the teaser rate period ended so that it did not matter if the mortgages they took out implied unaffordable payments in the future. However, when house prices stopped increasing, many people found they were unable to make the payments. As a result, they were facing repossession of their homes, and the mortgage issuers, such as HSBC, were facing default on the money owed.

The implications were that if house prices fell further HSBC would suffer additional and significant losses.

In the US, mortgages are non-recourse loans. This means that if you give the title of the house back to the mortgage lender, you have fulfilled all your liabilities and it does not matter if that house is now worth less than the amount of the loan you owed. There was no recourse back to you for the difference. This practice of dropping the keys to the bank and walking away from the difference is called 'jingle mail', due to the supposed sound of the keys dropping through the letterbox of your lender.

By June, other institutions were well on the way to issuing similar trading updates. The US housing market was imploding and as the news of this went out, people started to default on their mortgage payments even more. Many people had purchased multiple properties on the basis of a promised price gain which was clearly not going to happen, and they were not going to be able to afford the mortgage payments that were coming. Even those who could afford the mortgage payments were giving the houses back as they were no longer likely to make money on their purchases.

Bear Stearns, a medium-sized US investment bank, started to fail as a result later in 2007; this caused a substantial fall in global financial markets. Recovery came later that year as central banks cut interest rates and provided additional money to support the economy; the stock market ended up making new highs even as the actual economy was collapsing.

2008 saw the convergence of fantasy with reality. The financial markets collapsed as Lehman Brothers, a major US investment bank, went bankrupt in September. The fear at the time was that money would stop flowing: ATMs would stop working; wages would no longer be able to be paid; shops would no longer be able to transact; people with money in banks would lose all their savings. This fear then spread globally. In the UK, the British mortgage lender and savings bank Northern Rock collapsed. The entire Icelandic economy fell apart and the country went bankrupt; Germany faced significant problems with most of its banks; the French bank Société Générale was engulfed in a major trading scandal costing several billion euros. The Greek economy, with its banks impacted and with the European institutions all weakened, became hostage to political bargaining and the country's population was reduced to the verge of starvation.

This whole period became known as the Global Financial Crisis. The economy took a year or more to settle and bottom out and even longer to start recovering. Even over 10 years later at the start of the Coronavirus pandemic, the world had still not recovered fully and the stimulus measures from central banks and governments were still in place.

So what really happened to cause all this?

The sequence of events that led to it is a good example of what happens in a reflexive cycle and how in such cycles good ideas inevitably turn bad. Even though genuine efforts were made by many to do good and without anyone needing to be particularly greedy, the sheer aggregate scale of activities breached the planet's financial capacity. We just ran past the cliff edge without being aware of it.

George Soros is the investor who made reflexive cycles famous by breaking the Bank of England during the period around the European currency union. In this era, European politicians believed they could force international trade to equalise between countries so that no country would benefit more than another by controlling the currency exchange rate. As usual, the intention was good, but there was a fallacy. Trade happens between countries because each has something to offer to the others that the others did not have, and this is reflected in the exchange rates. Fixing the exchange rates does not change the advantages and skills of one country over another; as a result, central banks, which were charged to maintain the politically preferred levels of the exchange rates, found themselves with an impossible task. It was like holding back floodwater with a spoon and without the ability to do anything about the source of the floodwater.

In the end, one after another, the central banks in Europe capitulated. On 16 September 1992, a day now known as Black Wednesday, Soros made his fortune as the British government admitted the fallacy of its thinking and gave up on maintaining the exchange rates at their unsupportable levels. Soros' description of reflexivity is as follows:

> My conceptual framework is built on two relatively simple propositions. The first is that in situations that have thinking participants, the participants' views of the world never perfectly correspond to the actual state of affairs. People can gain knowledge of individual facts, but when it comes to formulating theories or forming an overall view, their perspective is bound to be either biased or inconsistent or both. That is the principle of fallibility.

> The second proposition is that these imperfect views can influence the situation to which they relate through the actions of the participants. For example, if investors believe that markets are efficient then that belief will change the way they invest, which in turn will change the nature of the markets in which they are participating (though not necessarily making them more efficient). That is the principle of reflexivity.

In the case of the Global Financial Crisis, the fallibility element was the belief that people bought houses as homes and distorted their perspective into viewing the whole mortgage market as 'safe as houses'. The second reflexivity element is that lending to facilitate house buying drives up house prices, creating a spur to further house buying and further house price increases.

There is generally an element of new technology involved to facilitate these cycles. New technology allows us to view the future with more optimism and permits us to proceed without our usual scepticism and caution. In the current climate, we very readily accept the promises of a new sustainable future which draws us into investing in technologies and solutions without having to think them through. The same happened in the Global Financial Crisis. The technological innovation then was financial, in the form of what was called a Collateralised Debt Obligation (CDO).

Government policy before the Global Financial Crisis encouraged home ownership. Governments still generally encourage home ownership. Politicians see this as being good for the people and can therefore increase their electoral support. Tax incentives are often used to offset the costs of mortgages, and special treatments are made available to help step on to the property ladder. When a home is purchased, there is generally a boost in spending coming from redecorating and modernising. All these aspects attract people who are working and have a regular income as the alternative of paying rent is often seen as an opportunity lost. To make home ownership happen, people borrow a large sum of money and pay it off in monthly instalments over 20 to 30 years.

At the other end of society, for retirees, the focus is to be able to draw on a regular pension. Pension funds face increasing liabilities as people live longer and need more for their care. Seeing this, the regulators put greater and greater pressure on pension trustees to demonstrate they have solutions in place to meet these long-term obligations to retirees. As a new retiree may well live for another

20 or more years, this means the pension industry is always on the lookout for opportunities that can guarantee regular payments over decades. Traditionally, this can come from governments who borrow to fund their public services and repay over a long time. Companies may be able to provide the same, but they, in general, cannot be trusted to remain in business over such a long horizon.

Mortgages are in some ways ideal because the homeowner is committed to repaying the loan over 20 to 30 years. However, the problem is that sometimes we cannot keep up with our mortgage payments. This may be because of the loss of a job, sickness, or other unexpected reasons. This means that although mortgages offer the possibility of long-term steady cash flows for the pension funds, the borrowers cannot be relied on individually to guarantee the payments.

In around 2000, novel financial engineering came about to regroup the payments from a large number of homeowners into pools of money. Each month, the money from a predetermined group of mortgages was gathered together. Some of the borrowers might have missed a payment, but the majority would have paid. Historically, people treated their houses as their homes, and have always prioritised making their mortgage payments ahead of paying other debts. So even if it was not possible to pinpoint who in a group would be or would not be able to make their mortgage payment in any particular month, it was very likely that the majority would make it. This could be expressed as an amount of money that would be collected with a high degree of certainty. If a thousand borrowers with 20-year mortgages were pre-selected for their payments to go into a pool, and each month we could be certain that money would be collected from at least 800 of them, and if each borrower paid $500 each month, then this would mean a minimum of $400,000 would be collected; this being $500 times the 800 borrowers who would make their payments. The pool could therefore offer a promise to a pension fund of $400,000 a month for 20 years. In return, the pension fund would pay the mortgage lender a lump sum upfront to 'buy' this stream of cash flows. This stream of cash flow is a 'CDO'.

The innovation was very favourably received by all parties. Pensions could now satisfy their regulators who demanded proof they had the cash flow available for the payments to the pensioners, and mortgage lenders could take profit upfront for the loans they were making. The home-seeking individuals were offered incentives to take out the mortgages, and governments were pleased by the increase in homeownership. It was a classic win-win situation. Financial technology had made it all possible.

What about the money from the other 200 of the 1,000 people in the pool that was not collected into the CDO? Many of these people probably would have made their payments also, and that should be of use in some way. If, say, we thought conservatively that up to half of these 200 people failed to make a payment, then that left a reasonable chance still of collecting another $50,000: $500 from each of 100 borrowers who did make their payments. This allowed the introduction of the 'CDO-squared'. If we took 10 such pools, then there was an almost certainty of collecting at least another $400,000. Eight such pools would have been sufficient, as eight times $50,000 would be $400,000; so, by requiring 10 such pools it would give us abundant room for error. We could therefore be very confident of guaranteeing another $400,000 to be sold as the next level of the CDO. This became structured as the CDO-squared and was offered to meet the pension liabilities again. Nothing was wasted.

The next step further was obvious. The remaining payments could further be gathered across a larger number of the CDO-squared pools, and structured into a 'CDO-cubed' to be sold.

Governments naturally encouraged the idea of home ownership, and regulations did not impede this growth. They only required that all these repackaged cash flows were rigorously stress-tested against different economic scenarios. If the country went into a recession, for example, people would have a greater risk of losing their income and would be less able to make their mortgage payments. Similarly, when people moved houses, their particular mortgages would be terminated as houses were sold and the loans paid off in full. The promised payments that stretched far into the future would then all be terminated. These effects needed to be modelled and that modelling was done. However, they missed out on essential elements which were impossible to anticipate.

As it became possible for a mortgage lender to sell off the cash flows and earn the fees without having to wait over 10, 20 or more years, it became attractive for more businesses to become mortgage lenders. As that happened, the typical competition for clients developed. Homeowners were being targeted to change from one mortgage lender to another, with financial incentives offered to do so, and as they refinanced their mortgages from one lender to take out a loan with another, it weakened the guarantees in the CDOs as the promised stream of payments was cut short.

There was more trouble on the way.

As long as we believe that owning a house meant treasuring the home we live in, buying houses and developing and building new homes is a good thing to encourage. Home ownership made economic sense, and the repackaging of the mortgage payments benefitted the pensioners. New homeownership led to a greater sense of wealth, and governments felt this also improved their electoral prospects. It was believed that house buying was good regardless of how it came about. This was the fallibility element of Soros's propositions. In America and the UK, house buying took off, funded by banks in their own countries and also by banks in Iceland, Ireland, Germany, Italy, and further afield.

The problem was there were far more people needing pensions than people stepping on the housing ladder, and so there were simply not enough mortgages. The solution was to encourage more mortgages, so people were encouraged to have second homes and holiday homes. The buy-to-let market where a property is purchased purely for rental purposes was developed. This opened up fantastic opportunities as house builders saw unlimited growth potential. There was no reason to think that families should be limited to having only one house; people could have as many properties as they wished. As this took off, house prices started to increase and as long as house prices increased, it did not matter if properties stood empty. The rising prices would cover the costs, and it became possible to borrow more than the value of a house to pay the mortgage for the first year or so. As more people raced to purchase more properties, house prices accelerated further even as new housing supplies grew.

This is the reflexivity element of Soros's proposition. The basis for lending is that house prices would not be affected by lending. However, as lending increased, it attracted more house buyers, causing house prices to rise. The more valuable houses became, the more businesses turned to mortgage lending. HSBC was one of the participants through its purchase of Household International. As more lenders entered the market, housing speculation and lending dominated the entire economies in countries such as Iceland and Ireland.

In America, over the space of a decade, houses began to be built and purchased in places where no one would previously have envisioned living. Property speculation became the only game in town. In this part of the reflexive cycle, we all think we have become great investors. House prices no longer had any bearing on income and other measures of value. Those houses that could not be rented stayed empty, but their prices rose all the same. Property investment became pure speculation, but one that was fully supported by governments, regulators, the financial industry, and most of all, by us, the people. Property purchases dominated everyday conversations. We all became the best marketers for further growth, as we all became experts at flipping houses.

In the end, so much debt was created that we simply exceeded the financial capacity of the planet. The belief that people cared intimately about the houses they owned and therefore always paid their mortgages before other debts proved to be wrong.

These reflexive cycles are common. We are very willing to overlook fallacies in our thinking and overestimate our ability to be rational in favour of flattering our investment acumen. Sustainability has many of the markings of such a cycle. The communication tactics of the recent past have emphasised an impending crisis and created an urgency to look to new technologies. With the promise of new technologies, we are led to believe in continual growth and enormous potential for profits. This is all blessed by governments and regulators and has a positive social value attached. It becomes a fallacy when we fail to verify if these efforts are genuinely beneficial to our physical world but accept that any effort is good. Vast sums of money are moving into this area. The disconnect between the timescale to demonstrate genuine progress and realising investment returns further encourages the reflexivity element. So far, the promised returns have clearly happened, but not the promised sustainability.

CHAPTER 8:

INVESTMENTS – THE AGE OF ASSET MANAGEMENT

More investments and better returns are not making the world better. The easier we make our money, the less respect we have for the world that has provided it.

Be more respectful; invest so that we live more fulfilling lives.

In April 2014, Andrew Haldane, the Chief Economist at the Bank of England and a member of its Monetary Policy Committee, gave a speech at the London Business School. The title of the speech was *The Age of Asset Management?*

The question was undoubtedly rhetorical, but the implication of the title is important; the size of investment assets is so large that everything in the world is defined by it. Haldane identified the size of the assets under management in 2014 as $87 trillion, and estimates today are that it has grown to over $100 trillion.

To give this number some context, the world produced 760 million tonnes of wheat in 2020, and the value of that quantity of wheat was not even close to $1 trillion. The 100 million or so new vehicles that are produced each year are worth only a few trillion dollars. All the gold in the world, including the bits in our jewellery and the ores in the ground yet unmined, only amounts to about $12 trillion as of October 2019. Savills, a leading global land and property agent estimated that all the agricultural and forestry land in the world in 2017 was worth about $27 trillion, and all the commercial real estate in the world comes to about $33 trillion. This is still a good way off the $100 trillion.

$100 trillion is a huge sum of money.

We may be surprised to find that this money is not the wealth of the super-rich. In 2020, PWC estimated the total wealth of people with more than $1 million as $76.9 trillion. This is separate from the $100 trillion mentioned earlier. The big guys set up private family offices and use special private investment vehicles to look after their money. The $100 trillion is money that is delegated to investment professions to manage in *collective investment pools*. These pools gather money from all of us. We contribute to them when we make payments into our pension plans or save into savings funds. They are also created when we take out life and similar insurance policies. Each of these collective investment pools has many people contributing to it, and each pool invests all the money in it as a single entity.

The money comes from our savings to provide for our own future. They may be for a rainy day, or for college fees. We may plan to finance a wedding or to contribute to a deposit on a house. Most of the money, though, is in our pension investments to provide us with an income when we retire.

As Haldane suggested, this money is changing the shape of the world we live in. For the first time in history, we the little guys with a total of over $100 trillion have more wealth than the big guys with their total of $76.9 trillion.

Three aspects of this money are important to appreciate. The first is how it got to be so large. The second aspect is that many of the things such as the exorbitant wealth of the super-rich, the demise of our high streets, our overconsumption, and short-termism in business that we bemoan are consequences of our demand for high investment returns. The last aspect is that the size of this money is now so large that we are running out of opportunities for sensible investments.

So how did it get to be so big?

Individual savings took off in the 1970s as governments realised that they were unlikely to have sufficient income to keep their promises of providing for our future. This led to a systematic move on the part of OECD governments to mandate individual investments. The OECD is the Organisation for Economic Co-operation and Development. It was the follow-on organisation to a group created for the Marshall Plan, a programme for development financed by the US to rebuild Europe after the Second World War, and consisted of a number of European countries with the intention of helping these countries to help each other. It has been credited with bringing about an era of co-operation that has lasted to today. When Brexit was being debated, one of the major benefits of the European Union was the absence of war on the continent for half a century. This lasting peace is considered as one of the results of that co-operation.

In 1961, Canada and the US formally joined the group and, by doing so, founded the OECD. The purpose, stated on the organisation's website, is to "achieve the highest sustainable economic growth and employment and a rising standard of living in member countries." Other countries were admitted over time.

Being admitted as a member is recognised as having reached the status of an economically developed country with high standards of human rights. Today, there are 37 members, and Colombia is the newest. It was admitted in April 2020. These countries are, by virtue of their membership, the most developed countries in the world, and it is important to point out that the goal of the group is still to promote further growth for themselves.

Most of the money in the collective investment pools Haldane noted come from savers in OECD countries. This money is the driving force behind the financialisation of our world, and, as an aside and to emphasise in case there is any doubt, all the damage caused by financialisation is therefore our own doing. The OECD countries' goal of attaining the 'highest sustainable growth' may sound good. In reality, we can never know if growth is ever sustainable or not. We are also rarely critical of ourselves when we appear successful. The goal of attaining the highest sustainable growth is therefore really no more than a euphemistic relabelling of the goal of achieving the highest growth.

Our investment philosophy aligns with this goal. It was always about generating the highest returns. The $100 trillion is saved and invested by us to provide for our future, and to ensure it will be sufficient for that purpose, we need it to grow at the highest possible rate. The highest economic growth and the highest investment returns are intimately linked. Our savings provide the capital that helps companies to expand, and companies expanding provides the profits that in turn grow our capital. To produce the highest returns for us, we need the kind of growth that focuses on money, which also happens to be the kind of growth that is easiest to achieve.

In the middle of the Second World War in 1942, Sir William Beveridge in the UK published a paper, *Social Insurance and Allied Services*, to advocate the abolition of the five evils: want, disease, ignorance, squalor and idleness. This set in motion the construction of the welfare state, offering to support all citizens by providing a public health service, better education, unemployment benefits, and state pensions. In the post-war period, other countries in Europe, and to a lesser extent the US, followed, with each country recognising that it was important its citizens could rely on their government for support. This led to an expansion of government and increased its need for taxation.

The 1970s, however, became a watershed moment. A report produced in the 1950s and kept secret for two decades was finally released by the US Committee on Foreign Relations in 1974. It revealed the persistent, immoral, illegal and economically ruinous practices that were carried out for decades by a cartel of seven western oil companies known as the Seven Sisters. The report was released just after the first oil shock, and it showed how these practices, supported implicitly by major western governments, ultimately backfired.

The oil-producing Arab states finally retaliated by using oil as a weapon in the Yom Kippur War. The price of oil tripled, and the supply to the West was dramatically cut. Signs of 'Sorry no gas' with lines of cars queuing became the defining image of the era. Even if you had the money, there was no gas to be bought. The impact was horrendous on economies that had come to treat energy and oil as limitless. As the economies collapsed, governments ran out of money. The UK government had to go begging, cap in hand, to the International Monetary Fund (IMF).

The IMF is basically a credit union, pooling contributions from its member countries to lend out to any of them who find themselves in a tight spot. Since countries in a tight spot generally have problems with their own finances, the IMF requires the borrower to implement policy changes to make sure that any money lent will be paid back. The borrowing countries, therefore, lose control of their domestic policies; so, depending on whether the country is a contributor or a borrower, the view of the IMF flips between that of a friendly banker or a nasty loan shark. The declassified Cabinet Minutes of the UK governments of the time showed how the IMF conditions required "cuts into public services so deep as to endanger their basic function and cuts in social benefits that would put at risk the Social Contract". These were the services that Beveridge had advocated for and achieved as part of the welfare state.

In the end, the UK government complied, and the economic reality was that even governments did not have limitless budgets. The subsequent loan had further knock-on effects; the amount needed was so large that even the IMF did not have enough money. It needed additional contributions from the US and Germany, which put further pressure on their budgets at a time when every country was financially hard pressed.

This also happened at a time when the average age of the population in developed countries was beginning to get higher. The future was going to be more retirees and fewer active workers, and the social funding for health, employment support, welfare, and state pensions was all provided out of tax revenues. The money that governments took in as taxes was paid out to fund social welfare and was used to pay back debts that had been taken out previously. Pensions were particularly important because every worker would eventually retire, and even those who had not worked would require some income in their old age.

As the number of people in the working population dropped, the amount of income from taxation would also drop. Governments realised they will eventually have to renege on their promises to look after their citizens. They began to shift the responsibility for long-term care back to individuals and incentives were created to encourage this transition. Tax breaks were introduced for contributions to private pensions and regulations tightened for collective investment pools to ensure that they were safe.

In 1974, the US implemented the *Employee Retirement Income Security Act* (ERISA). This marked the start of a new era. Before this, similar investment pools frequently collapsed and people who had money invested in them lost their savings. The US government recognised that individuals would only save if they were sure their savings were secure. However, rather than guaranteeing the savings, the act made it illegal for the collective investment pools to put anything other than the interests of the savers first. This was expressed explicitly as focusing on obtaining the highest possible returns. In the decade that followed, the number of private pension plans in the US doubled as confidence in them grew. In a recent June 2020 proposal, the US Department of Labour, in the light of the debates on sustainability, again restated the duty of these investment pools as achieving the best returns.

As mentioned in an earlier chapter, Schroders, a large asset manager, did a global study of 23,000 investors from 32 countries to find out what they were expecting in terms of returns from their savings over the next five years. It categorised investors by country and found that investors in over half of the countries expected a return of more than 10.9% per year. On the $100 trillion of assets, 10.9% return translates to $11 trillion of profit for the first year and increasing through compounding as the gains are accumulated to a total gain of over $68 trillion. Even if some of this money will be spent by us when we use our savings, we will still be making new contributions, and it is likely that we will be well on our way to doubling what we have now in the space of only five years.

This $11 trillion of profit for the first year in the context of the OECD countries means squeezing an average of $18,000 from each worker. The OECD countries have 605 million full-time and part-time workers across the 37 countries and the average full-time salary in 2019 was $48,587. Going through this country by country, for Mexico which has the lowest full-time salary at $17,594, we will take all the salaries from every full-time working Mexican, and they will still be owing to us a little bit. Eight countries have an average full-time salary in the $20,000s, and here it will be sufficient if they all hand over their earnings to our portfolios. Because this is the gross salary, that is the salary before any tax is paid, we are also taking from all their governments.

With no income tax revenues, we are also taking away their social welfare, public infrastructure and, of course, their state pensions. Six countries have an average salary in the $30,000s, seven in the $40,000s, nine in the $50,000s, and at the top, four have a full-time average salary in the $60,000s. The top position is occupied by Luxembourg at $68,681. From these workers in Luxembourg, we would be requiring over 37% of their after-tax income. This analysis may seem facetious, but it gives food for thought as to why we are paid the way we are.

Alternatively, we can seek these gains from the other 6 billion or so people in the world in countries not in the OECD. This has been the thinking behind the high-growth businesses over the past decade, breaking into the populations of China, India, South East Asia, South America, the Middle East, and Africa. Of course, to make it work, pretty much all the gains will still have to come to us. As an example, according to Paylab.com, the salary for a shop assistant in Malawi is only about $2,500 a year, and the number is similar in Nigeria. Because these numbers are so low, we can even claim to be generous to enhance our image.

As we exploit the land, dig up the resources, burn the forests, we can include a modest pay rise for those living there and still be able to walk off with sufficient profits to add meaningfully to our $11 trillion target. This can continue for as long as we like, so long as we do not allow their income levels to come anywhere close to ours. Again, if this seems facetious, Rio Tinto is one of our largest mining companies, and they put out a video to promote their social contribution on Twitter in May 2020. This highlighted their contribution of $120 million in taxes and royalties to Africa as a demonstration of the social good they do. The $120 million for Africa is 3.3% of the value of the company's non-current assets in the continent based on their 2019 annual report. The non-current assets are dominated by basically the tangible things the company owns, so this basically suggests Rio Tinto pays a rent of 3.3% to Africa to mine the resources. In contrast, $6.2 billion or 82% of the taxes and royalties Rio Tinto pays is paid to the company's home country, Australia; this corresponds by the same measure to a 22% rent in their home country. However we would like to think of our social responsibilities, we still tend to treat ourselves better.

Simply, to make our profits, we take them from where we can. We have always done it this way, and this is the way we will keep doing it if this is the kind of returns we need.

The finance industry would argue that there is another way that this can come about; that is for things to become more pricey. The stock market can double in value, and with it, our houses can also double in value. We may need to pay double for our meals and education to support the idea that things are worth twice as much. This would help to double the value of the companies we have in our portfolios.

Equally, our expectations for profits in the future can also double. However, our salaries would need to stay more or less the same. Otherwise, we would be taking away the profits we are hoping for, and prevent us from achieving the $11 trillion. So, we will all feel more financially squeezed even as our portfolios get more valuable. Is this at all reminiscent of how we may have been feeling in the past decade?

In the end, the money that makes up the $100 trillion comes from us and we demand it to grow to meet our increasing needs. The necessary returns can be generated, but the outcomes may not provide us with the better future we are hoping for. Ironically, when we aim for high returns, we make our future less secure. This is because the reflexive cycles we explained are triggered by high returns. The more we use finance to ensure our future, the more it tends to impact the world by financialising it. Although it is not necessarily the case that the impact has to be bad every time, it generally is, because to make the real world better takes time and patience, and time and patience are anathemas to high financial returns.

The second point is that the problems of wealth inequality and the damages to our communities that we bemoan and regret are largely from our own doing. They are the consequences of us having lots of money chasing and achieving high investment returns. These damages come about as a result of reflexive cycles and are the consequences of actions that we believe to be good. It is the downside of the Age of Asset Management.

By 2013, the Global Financial Crisis had by and large passed. Growth had recovered. The economies of the US, UK, and Japan each grew by about 2%, while Germany's economy managed over 0.4%. China, which had been providing the global economy with growth, was mellowing, but its economy still managed growth of over 7%. The employment situation around the world was improving. With job creation brisk, the picture was rosy.

However, growth was still regarded as low. This was because it was being compared with the peak years before the crisis. One of the aspects of chasing the *highest* growth is that it encourages us to try to beat previous records. Central banks across Europe, UK, Japan and the US kept interest rates near zero and even negative to force more economic activities. Governments increased their fiscal spending, even while they were sending a message of austerity to manage expectations. These stimulus policies achieved their goal of increasing financial speculation.

E-commerce and disruptive technologies found a ready audience. Disruptive technologies are technologies that enable businesses like Amazon to *disrupt* our traditional retail industries. Airbnb is an example that undercuts hotels and lodgings; Uber challenges traditional taxi services; Google and Facebook infiltrate advertising. They do so by claiming to be technologies and not services, and therefore they can operate without the costs of having to comply with existing regulations.

Against this backdrop, any business that could be relabelled as a technology business was indeed relabelled as a technology business. If you put an 'e-' to the name of a business, the value of that business immediately increased. This created a niche for businesses that performed the same functions as traditional ones but did not have to pay the regulatory costs that centuries of hard-fought struggles against exploitation had established. This is clearly bad for us, but marketing and the appeal of the new allowed them to be sold as innovations with promises of a new economy and untold profits. Our money found its way in droves into these ventures.

In 2013, Jim Cramer, the host of CNBC's boisterous Mad Money commentary programme on financial markets, pitched the term FANG to capture the technology companies that represented the future. These were Facebook, Amazon, Netflix and Google, with their initials spelling the word FANG. The share prices of these companies had been moving unrelentingly higher as people bought into their stories. As more of their shares were bought, more interest in their stories developed driving the prices up further.

These four companies came to be worth more and more, and by conventional understanding, their relative weight in the economy has also increased. Existing, traditional businesses were, *de facto*, losing out because they had proven profitability which anchored our expectations. The new businesses, however, had no profits. Their business model was to promote growth above all else and any revenues were spent to push for further expansion. This allowed people to entertain flights of fancy as to their future worth.

At the same time, according to a BIS report, about 12% of investment assets were tracking pre-selected benchmark indices of companies. These indices are typically created according to a formula, the most common of which is an index of all companies weighted in the ratio of how much each company is worth. The value of a company is readily reflected in their stock prices and is known as its market capitalisation.

So if there were two companies, SuperStock and SpeedyStock, and you did not know which is a better one to invest in, this approach would say own them both but in the proportion of how big they are. If SuperStock is twice the size of SpeedyStock in terms of how much the companies are worth, then split your money so you have twice the amount invested in SuperStock as the amount invested in SpeedyStock.

The reason behind this allocation method is that people who know about these companies and their prospects are on the lookout for any information that will be pertinent to how well or poorly these companies will do. When something happens that affects the outlook of a company, these people will work through the details to understand what the information will mean for the company's prospects and revenues now and in the future. They will then adjust their estimates of the value of the company accordingly. If the new estimates are higher than what the current share price may be suggesting, this will motivate them to purchase more shares at the current cheaper price. This will nudge the price up until the company is considered to be no longer underpriced. Conversely, if the new estimates suggest the company is now overvalued, they would be motivated to sell the shares. Because there are investors who actively study companies, the prices of shares are always adjusting to their best estimated values.

The important relation here is that the estimated value of the company should reflect the market capitalisation. If what you want to do then is to invest across all companies in a way that stays consistent with how active investors are investing, then the answer is to divide your money in proportion to the companies' individual market capitalisation. So, passive investing means piggybacking on the work of active investors. To do otherwise means you have some reason to believe you know better. Benchmark investing, which is also known as passive investing, is generally recommended and accounts for a very large and rising portion of regular investment contributions. The approach relies on a firm belief that there are active investors out there doing their jobs.

As the share prices of the FANGs rose, the weights of the four companies as a proportion of the market increased, and more and more money from our savings contributions were allocated to them through passive investing. Active managers who had discretion not to follow the market benchmarks and considered the increased valuations too high lost out. As they underperformed, they were punished by investors with redemptions. As a result, we steadily moved away from investing in active managers who did their own research and moved into passive funds which simply followed.

In June 2019, the investment research company Morningstar pointed out that the size of assets under passive management in the US equalled the amount under active management. This was surpassed a few months later. When there is more money under passive management than active management, our understanding that prices are determined by those who are doing the work for us becomes a fallacy. What started off as a sensible practice became corrupted; we bought more FANG stocks simply because each contribution we made to our investments pushed the prices higher. Without the active investors correcting their prices, the higher prices prompted us to buy more of the same next time.

This created a reflexive cycle and led to a financial bubble in the FANG stocks. The impact of it continued with a transformation into the real economy. These reflexive excesses never leave the real economy without damage, but we see the impacts as affirmations of our own successes in predicting the e-commerce and disruptive technology successes.

Amazon out-competed traditional bricks and mortar shops, pushing them to reduce their high street presence. We switched from making shopping trips to receiving next day or same day deliveries. The look of the high streets started to change. These became proof that the investment idea was right, and the future was in e-commerce.

However, it did not happen just because our demands moved this way. It happened because Amazon is one of the biggest advertising spenders in the world. In 2019, it ranked number one, spending $11 billion or over $30 million dollars a day on advertising. It invested hugely to make sure we were directing our shopping to its site. Once we were on the site, technology was used extensively to cross-sell related products and up-sell higher value products to us. Our shopping baskets were analysed for better personalised targeting to make these sales strategies less noticeable.

The familiar high street shops were condemned for not having this kind of advertising power, and as Amazon's advertising attracted more businesses away from them, their situation became worse. As the bricks and mortar businesses pay local taxes and employ local people, with their demise we also lost the funding and infrastructure to our local communities. The reflexive cycle resulted in a self-reinforcing success of e-commerce over the demise of traditional retail, driven by our investments in the e-commerce companies.

Future profits from e-commerce are also greater because e-commerce does not need to pay the taxes and rates that traditional retailers pay, and they can employ people without the cost burden of having to provide the employment benefits that our high street shops need to provide. The profits are also greater because the technologies they use actually work to promote more consumption. E-commerce creates more shopping. A study by Duch-Brown *et al* at the European Commission's Joint Research Centre shows that having online sales increased total sales, even as offline sales decreased. The combination of advertising, technology and convenience prompts us to buy more without us realising.

Alibaba is a Chinese online retailer similar to Amazon. It operates mainly in Asia and has been promoting a Single's Day shopping festival. This has become the largest shopping event in the world, and it happens each year on 11 November. When this is written as 11.11, it is a series of single digits, hence its name. It was started not as a shopping event, but as a day of celebration for people who are not in a relationship, analogous to Valentine's Day for couples.

In 2019, $1 billion of sales happened in the first minute of the Single's Day event; 544,000 orders per second were created during the busiest part of the day. In total $38.4 billion of transactions were made, and they generated over 1.8 billion deliveries. In 2020, the same event achieved twice the total value of sales.

The 1.8 billion deliveries generated actually do need to be delivered. Conway and Browne examined online shopping and identified a significant increase in urban congestion due to online sales related to delivery traffic. The congestion is a collective knock-on effect. The delivery van itself only adds a little to the traffic, but when it stops on the side of the road, as we have all experienced, cars behind it are forced to slow down or to stop, creating little bubbles of congestion that drag more cars into it. The effect of congestion, aside from the inconvenience, is also more fuel use and more pollution.

Richard Driscoll looked into travel mileage in the US between 2009 and 2017 and found that total mileage increased with the increase coming from service trips. Service trips are journeys made by delivery vans and new car-share services like Uber and Lyft. They added to the existing traffic without creating a corresponding drop in overall household travel mileage. What happened is that all the convenience just went into giving us more time to spend on other trips. These additional trips we made also added to the overall increase in congestion.

One more scary ramification of continually increasing our travel mileage in the US is reported by Lambert *et al* in October 2020's edition of *Geophysical Research Letters*. In the US, gasoline has to have a biofuel component. This was originally introduced to help slow climate change. More traffic means more biofuel. Biofuel is made from crops like soy and corn, and these crops are grown through a process known as monocropping. By a combination of genetic engineering and pesticide use, massive areas of farmlands grow a single crop with no other plants present. Bio-engineering is used to create glyphosate-tolerant crops; glyphosate is a systemic weedkiller that kills all other plants. The result is vast fields where the only plants growing are soy and corn. Since soy and corn crops are annual crops, they die off after each growing season and cannot help to retain soil.

Years of this practice has led to significant soil degradation and loss. The physical impact is an abundance of dust as the loose soil is picked up by winds, and this dust is now being associated with the emergence of new Dust Bowl events. The occurrences of severe dust storms have picked up from Colorado to Kansas in a repeat of the first Dust Bowl events of the 1930s. The dust particles become fine particles of air pollution and damage health.

Monocropping is also identified as contributing to a devastating reduction in insect populations. The loss of all other plant life has meant that plants that form essential habitats for many insects no longer exist. Among the insects affected, the monarch butterfly stands out because of its incredible life cycle. The butterfly overwinters in Mexico, making a 3,000-mile migratory flight from north to south along the American continent. Once they reach Mexico, they begin to breed a new generation. This then makes its progress back northwards in a series of smaller hops of several hundred miles each with a new generation born at each hop. Each generation lives for only a few weeks, and the final generation that makes the astounding journey back to Mexico has remarkably never seen the country before. The butterflies feed on milkweed, and as a result of monocropping, this plant is now so scarce that the population of the butterfly has reduced by between 80% to 99% since 1980.

The impact of our investments is not limited to the pressures on the physical world. As early as 2003, research was showing issues emerging on the societal side. Things like privacy rights, consumer protection and workers' benefits were all being eroded. On top of this, Amazon, for example, has barely been profitable despite its growth and its huge valuation. This meant it has not needed to pay any tax. The promise of greater profit for our investments is depleting our governments of the taxes traditional retailers pay. Our governments lose out on their ability to balance the public budget, putting pressure to increase income and other taxes.

These are some of the observations of what happens when our investments cause reflexive cycles. To finish off, we go back to the super-rich and look at how they got here.

The share price of Amazon grew by a factor of 10 over the past decade and that of the FAANGs as a group (Apple was later included to give it the second A) grew by 900% between 2013 to October 2020. According to Institutional Asset Manager, these companies now represent about 15% of the US equity market. With this astronomical return, they alone would account for a 150% rise in the US equity market over the same period. That is, if $10,000 were invested into Amazon in 2013, it would now be worth $100,000. If $10,000 were invested broadly across all the public companies in the US, the rise in the price of the FAANG stocks alone would make the investment worth $25,000. This has made Amazon not only a great story for our pensions and for our individual investments, but it also made Jeff Bezos, the founder, one of the richest men alive.

In November 2020, Jeff Bezos was actually ranked as the richest person in the world with a worth of $181 billion. $160 billion of this is from the 54,474,763 shares he held in his company. We as investors also hold shares in Amazon, as we are the owners of 84.9% of the company. This ownership gives us a wealth of $1.3 trillion. So Jeff Bezos is wealthy in the same way that our investment portfolios are wealthy, and it came about because we have been buying shares in the company passively.

The remaining $20 billion of Jeff Bezos's wealth has come from him selling his shareholdings in the company. These shares are largely bought with our money as we add to our investment savings. Each time we make a contribution to our savings or pension plans, he sells a few of his shares to us. In the run-up to the 2020 US Presidential election, he sold 899,191 shares. This is less than 2% of the 54 million shares he held, but he banked $2.7 billion in cash from it.

Forbes lists 2,095 billionaires in the world in 2020, and their aggregate worth is about $8 trillion. Most of this wealth, as in the case of Jeff Bezos, is wealth in the companies they are associated with. They have become wealthy because our investments have elevated the value of their companies. We have done this to improve the value of our investment portfolios, and as a by-product, we have created the class of the super-rich.

In our discussions on the Global Financial Crisis, we mentioned that government and regulatory policies encouraged the development of the property bubble, and in earlier chapters, we described how intervention became the way to ensure growth. In the decade since the Global Financial Crisis, the prolonged low, zero, and even negative interest rate policies have created a sense for the investment manager of 'there is no alternative' or TINA. This is a sense that in the face of the unrelenting rise of the shares, not participating even if it is wrong to participate will only leave your own performance so far behind that it becomes unacceptable. There is therefore no alternative but to join in. So, from the end of the crisis to about the middle of 2016, before the Trump election, the only way to meet the pressures of producing returns was to buy into rising share prices, even if they seemed expensive.

When Trump was elected as US President at the end of 2016, sentiment changed to believing in a resurgence of unbridled capitalistic growth. This prompted the sense of FOMO, that is, the fear of missing out. Trump made people feel it was OK to do whatever we wanted to do. Regulations that protected society were to be revoked. Taxes would be lowered, and there would be money to spend. It did not matter if all this speculation hurt our neighbours, and even in this environment of high expected growth, central banks injected still more money into the system.

Investment managers generally take the attitude that if they do not get in on an opportunity, then someone else would anyway, leading to the spirit of leaving nothing on the table. So in the end they may as well be the ones to go first and reap a bit of benefit for themselves and hopefully for their clients. This is fundamental to the mandates they work under. If they underperform their peers, then they are out of a job.

As Trump's presidency progressed and FOMO took over, stocks began to make new all-time highs. Benchmarked investing became the safest approach and provided the highest returns. All this made those who had assets rich, or at least their investment portfolios rich. It also turned the founders of companies, especially the founders of the companies that promised a new economy, into the super-rich. The stimulus from the Coronavirus pandemic has promoted this further, with an expectation that policymakers will do their utmost to recover the growth that has been lost. Even the Japanese stock market, which since its collapse at the end of the 1980s had languished for decades, made a new high after 31 years on 14 January 2021. The cycle has made the rich become richer, and it has done so because of the shares we bought to propel them to their riches in just the same way that our buying has added to our own financial wealth. However, the growing inequalities this has created is leaving us feeling troubled.

Ironically, when these elements of policy and high return expectations work together to ensure our future but create reflexive cycles, our future becomes more uncertain. While we may succeed in gaining nominal wealth, what we can genuinely achieve with that wealth is rapidly lost. Just like in the California Gold Rush, money did not bring about the certainties it promised.

This brings us back to our pension funds' ownership of vineyards, and the third of our points: how the size of the investment assets is now changing the purpose of real activities like farming and housing.

First, we need to sidestep into some finance and explain portfolio allocation. The question here is what we should invest in, and in what proportions. The starting point is to clarify the different choices for investments. Then we can see how to calculate their right proportions. The relevance of all this is to explain how mathematics leads us into investing in things like vineyards for our investment portfolios. Of course, spoiler alert, we will conclude with the fact that the size of our investment assets is so large that this venturing into real assets is damaging.

Traditional assets are equities and bonds. Equities are about investing in the companies as owners and sharing their profits. Bond investments mean lending money, typically for the long term and to very good credit entities like governments. Generally, this is to the G7 governments, and most of the lending is to the US government.

Equity investments help companies to raise more capital and improve their profile, and in principle, as owners of the shares, it gives us the right to determine their business policies. Bond investments help governments to buffer their finances, especially in times when income from taxation is low, so that public works may continue. Our investment money, therefore, serves to help our society to develop, at least in principle. In practice, this growth is sensible only if the risks are somewhat symmetric. That is, if you made an error of judgment then you would face losses, just as if you were right in your judgment then you would reap benefits. Unfortunately, the reality is different. The exercise of caution has become punished and the pursuit of recklessness is rewarded as regulators and policymakers strive to promote growth.

When the economy is doing well, there are many equity opportunities as companies generally do well. If economic growth is projected to slow, then the outlook for companies worsens. The appetite for equity investments wanes. At the same time, guaranteed payments from governments with strong credit become more attractive, and the demand for bonds generally increases. Such a change in outlook will push the price of equities down and drive the price of bonds up. For a portfolio holding both equities and bonds in some combination, their opposing price movements provide a stabilising influence on the total valuation. The classic proportion is to consider 60% invested in equities and 40% invested in bonds; the actual proportions may vary somewhat.

At the time of the Global Financial Crisis, equities lost more than half of their value and all portfolios suffered large losses regardless of their mix of equities and bonds. At the time, analysis into commodities suggested that the prices of agricultural commodities moved differently and were not subject to the same investment forces. This was because they were responding to things like the trends in food consumption and the changes in the weather, and were less influenced by the state of our economy. After all, everyone needs to eat even in a financial crisis, and droughts happen whether the economy is booming or not.

Managers of pensions, insurance companies and mutual funds started to look seriously into these assets, in particular into things like farmland, forestry, and real estate. Agribusiness became an asset class for financial investments.

The story for investing in real assets was made even stronger by the central banks' stimulus actions. The received wisdom is that when money printing happens, inflation runs wild. This is largely taken from the experience of the Weimar Republic after the First World War when rampant inflation followed government policies of money printing to pay wages and debt. The stimulus measures following the Global Financial Crisis were considered as amounting to money printing by many, and there was a good chance in the minds of economists and investment professionals that such actions would cause high inflation. If this were to happen, then the prices for real goods would escalate. Investing in agriculture and farmland therefore provided protection, as these too would escalate in value. Furthermore, the high octane areas of e-commerce and disruptive technologies were likely to do really poorly in such situations, as only physical goods would retain value. Farms produced real produce, and what could be better than that?

With traditional assets, experience through trial and error had established that the allocation mix of 60% investment to equities and 40% to bonds is good. Farm assets were new additions, and new calculations were needed to find the right proportions. Back in 1952, an economist, Harry Markowitz, came up with a *Modern Portfolio Theory*, which allowed an investor to determine the optimal mix between any assets. He was later awarded the Nobel Prize in Economics in recognition of this achievement. His paper *Portfolio Selection* provided a straightforward computational procedure to determine this optimal mix, and in the 70 plus years since its first publication, the approach has become the scientific foundation to portfolio allocation.

The principle is that a portfolio with a better anticipated return and lower anticipated risks is more 'efficient', and therefore should be preferred over a portfolio with either a poorer anticipated return or higher anticipated risks. The rest is simply to iterate through all the possible combinations of the assets to find the ones that had a good ratio of anticipated return to anticipated risks. At Markowitz's time in the 1950s, computers were available but scarce, and running complex computation programs was very expensive. A simplified way was to calculate the returns for each potential asset separately and estimate the correlation in their price movements to deduce their optimal mix. This approach became known as the mean-variance approach.

Today, Nuveen, one of the largest agribusinesses, optimises its farmland portfolio by following this procedure. The inputs are the price histories of row crops in Illinois, Mississippi, Australia, Brazil, Poland, and Romania, and the price histories of almonds, pistachios, and Cabernet Sauvignons in the US. With these, they can look across all combinations to decide how much investment in each is needed.

The calculation of how farm produce can be incorporated into investment portfolios showed that they can improve the stability of returns. However, we have over $100 trillion worth of financial investments, and the value of the crops as food is only worth a few trillion dollars. For the results of this calculation to be effective, we need a lot more contributions from agriculture to our investment portfolios. The result is that the corporate agribusinesses we invest in need to own more farmland so that they are able to produce the size of the income we need.

The source of the problem is that the risks highlighted by Markowitz were financial risks, and not unquantifiable risks like the damage to our world if we financialised food production. It led us to think that 'portfolio optimisation' provided a solution when in fact it sustained a fallacy. The fallacy is that we can always achieve our investment returns without damaging our planet if we looked hard enough.

There are now many organisations worldwide seeking to protect the family farmer against the encroachment of agribusinesses. The primary motivation is to preserve the productivity of the land. With family-owned farms, the land is a multi-generational, perpetual asset. The owning family is motivated to maintain the land's quality as an asset for all generations and not for its financial value. In contrast, agribusinesses, even if it is 'far-sighted', still needs to value the farmland on a transactional basis in terms of what it will sell for. They have to do what is economically right with their assets and sell them either to take profit on their investments or to sell them before risks of significant financial losses become realised.

Actionaid USA, the American arm of an international network for building a just, equitable, and sustainable world, reports how farms in Iowa used to plant on average over 30 different types of crops when it's now two: corn and soy. Corn and soy are the two most consistently profitable crops because of their policy mandated use in biofuel. The consequence is a reduction of agricultural diversity, leading to topsoil erosion, and so on. Since the focus on corn and soy is the production of ethanol for biofuel, this creates in turn a vested economy through our other investments to maintain a dependency on biofuel use in transportation.

GRAIN, an organisation that supports small farmers to maintain community control and protect biodiversity-based farming, further highlights how this financialisation of farming affects countries across the world. The move to farmland investing is aided by its popularisation among investment professionals. The creation of the NCREIF farmland total return index has created an easily followed reference for passive farmland performance and promoted the asset class into mainstream investing. These businesses have pushed up the price of farmland, and the result is more land is made into farmland. It means that agriculture is being developed beyond the need for food sufficiency, to becoming principally a provider of stability to financial portfolios.

Mauro Armelin, the executive director of Amigos da Terra Amazônia Brasileira, an NGO, commented with reference to deforestation, "Even if no sugarcane is planted in the next five years in the Amazon... there will be land appreciation, leading the agricultural frontier deeper into the forest, where the land grabbers are..." Sugarcane in Brazil, incidentally, is a highly desirable row crop because it is used as biofuel locally, whereas soy and other row crops are exported as feedstock or food. The price dynamic is therefore quite different, and this makes it highly desirable in portfolio construction. Once again, it is desirable because it helps to meet our expectations for consistent and high returns for our investment portfolios.

In addition to farmlands, real estate investments have also become a significant part of the pension and investment portfolios. Prequin, a research company specialising in alternative investments, estimated that $1 trillion was deployed in 2016 by pension funds in this area. The investments are both direct, as in the funds become the property developers or the rental landlords, or indirect by investing into entities that perform those roles for them. The focus is often to capitalise on demand from the millennials and the middle-income renter markets, which is a sector that can afford higher rents. Deutsche Wohnen, which is owned by our investment money and includes some of the most ethically managed pension funds, is a major landlord in cities like Berlin.

This move into residential properties has distorted the housing supply so much that the Berlin government moved to freeze rent in an effort to keep its city centre affordable to its ordinary residents. At the same time, the move by investment funds to venture into residential properties is encouraged, as providing housing supply is seen as much needed. In the end, financial investments seek returns. Rabobank pension fund's €2.3 billion property portfolio, for example, returned 12.4% per year between 2016 and 2018. As long as the returns are good, the risk for reflexive feedback that ends up damaging housing affordability is an acceptable price to pay.

The age of asset management is an age of financialisation. With $100 trillion of assets to deploy and growing, there is no end of harm our money can do.

CHAPTER 9:

SUSTAINABLE INVESTING

Sustainable investing should be about outcomes and not about profits.

Don't let our investment managers be rewarded before we have seen the outcomes.

Sustainable investing is now the biggest trend in investment management. Given the impact investments have on our world, a trend specifically focusing on sustainability deserves attention, and we give an introduction to it here.

The investment industry has always been concerned with our economic and social situations. It naturally adapts to factors that drive our businesses and, because of this, nothing escapes the industry. Everything is part of the economic system and is either the result of or in need of investments. It is therefore an industry that would be adapting to the sustainability transition regardless of whether there are explicit policy directives to do so or not. This makes the current promotion of sustainable investments pure marketing.

The transformation in the industry has been to promote three pillars: environmental, social and governance. These are shortened into the acronym ESG. In the past decade or so, it has been more concerned with the environmental aspects as the climate issues are seen as having the greatest implications to the way we live. They therefore offer the greatest promise of a new economy. However, as a result of the Coronavirus pandemic, the social aspects are growing. The area that is seriously missing attention is governance. This is actually the most important area if we are to consider having genuine voices to shape how we want the businesses we own to operate. The problem today is that our voices as the owners of the money are displaced by those of investment managers. The governance area is especially rife with conflicts of interests. In the end, those who speak loudest in the industry tend to be those with the most vested interests.

The actual investment approaches may be divided into three broad categories. The first is known as impact investing. This engages in projects that directly seek to address specific development goals. These projects have a long history, and many have existed way before the idea of ESG investment ever hit the screens and were often part of the UN's development agenda. More recently, the goals have been relabelled in terms of the UN's 17 Sustainable Development Goals (SDGs) and their 169 targets. The investments are varied, and they can be large or small, touching on areas from forestry and farming techniques to mobile banking and satellite communications.

The second category is risk mitigation. This asks if an investor with a financial portfolio is sufficiently aware of how much the value of the portfolio may be at risk due to ESG factors, such as global warming scenarios or workplace diversity-driven changes. This means, for example, knowing about how much an investment in an insurance company may lose if flooding due to climate change becomes more frequent.

On a portfolio level, it is asking the extent to which investing in battery technology, which may benefit from the efforts to mitigate climate change, may help to offset the potential losses from holding shares in the said insurance company with the losses arising from increased incidences of severe flooding as a result of climate change. As the examples suggest, the focus here is less about achieving sustainability, but more about preserving the financial value of our investment portfolios.

Financial regulators and policymakers have been very vocal about the risks to the economic value of our portfolios. This is because there are significant risks to our overall economic stability if our investment portfolios end up with substantial losses. If we were to lose vast sums of money from our investment savings, then our retirement futures will be put at risk, putting pressures on much of our social infrastructure. The funding for old age is simply not present without our investment portfolios. Much of what is underlying this call for risk mitigation is therefore the desire to be able to continue with our economic growth path.

The third category is performance seeking by altering our business profiles to achieve a sustainability transition in our physical world. This is what the majority of sustainable marketing is promoting. The idea is by selecting those companies which have good sustainability practices and deselecting those which are considered as bad actors, we will serve both goals of enhancing our performance and saving the world.

Investment management would naturally have considered the risk mitigation and the sustainability transition aspects as part of its normal day-to-day business. The sentiments are, however, that we need to accelerate the pace. That has created the explicit labelling of investment products as sustainable, so they may be held up to be counted. Those investment products which do not carry such labelling will be crossed off instead. The danger is as more money enters the space, there will be a greater focus on financial returns instead.

All these categories of investing require data, including data on every business and project in the world. This is a major undertaking. However, as more money becomes involved, more and more data companies are attracted, and the growth of that data is more assured.

The information that is needed in each of these three investment categories is different. For impact investing, with its longer timescale and more explicit goals, there is a more established science behind the gathering of evidence with actual verification of benefits versus harm. These efforts are frequently linked with academic studies as the original projects were more experimental in nature. Surveys are used and a high degree of follow-up is usual. However, with more investors moving into sustainable investing, there is likely to be a problem with the timescale differences between the long-time horizons needed to verify that environmental or social goals are realised and the much shorter time horizons in which we expect financial returns to be achieved.

If we consider tree planting, for example, the true timescale is not when the saplings are planted or when the seeds are sown, but decades later to see if the trees have grown. Furthermore, we should consider if growing trees in one area has not pushed deforestation into other areas. Such an alignment of return incentive with actual impact would mean the investor should not be paid out until the end of several decades, and would not be paid if the benefits were not found. This obviously is not what most investors have in mind.

The story of sustainable investing is that returns will not suffer. The *UBS Wealth Management Webpage* on sustainable and impact investing has a 'myth vs reality' section, and the first myth to be dispelled is 'You sacrifice performance'. It states evidence that it is to the contrary, that sustainable investments improve your returns. This is now universally accepted as true. However, what the data really shows is that investments in the group of opportunities that are labelled as sustainable have outperformed. What it has not shown is that investments in these opportunities have produced a sustainable world. It has also not tried to demonstrate in any scientific manner that continued investments in these opportunities will bring about a sustainable world. The investment industry is not about science, it is about providing high returns. Your performance may not need to be sacrificed can simply be because the investments may not produce sustainability in any real sense.

The Norwegian government's efforts in this area are interesting because they show how a thorough audit of sustainable efforts is needed if we want to know if our investments are actually beneficial or not. In 2018, their Office of the Auditor General published the result of an investigation into the country's International Climate and Forest Initiative. The Storting, the supreme legislature of the country, allocated NOK 23.6 billion, roughly $2.5 billion, over a 10-year period from 2008 to an initiative to preserve tropical forests in developing countries. The goal of the investigation was to assess whether the investment created effective means of reducing greenhouse gas emissions from deforestation and forest degradation in the targeted countries.

The report pointed to serious issues. Conflicts of interest with changing political priorities created obstacles to the implementation of the policy; payment delays eroded trust in it; logging relocation was common, where deforestation was apparently stopped to benefit from payments from the scheme but continued outside of the banned areas to benefit from commercial exploitation, and highlighted the difficulty in getting people to turn down commercial interests; there was a general lack of effort to generate sustained funding, putting the longevity of the projects at risk. The report also noted the lack of consideration for the safeguarding of local communities and significant risks of fraud.

This audit exercise pointed out how our focus on sustainability makes us prone to *hypothesis myopia*. This is the tendency to collect evidence only about one hypothesis, and in the extreme but common form only the evidence that supports the hypothesis. This is why the Norwegian government's initiatives were not successful. If we only look at the evidence that supported the creation of a safe zone for forests, then we would have concluded, wrongly, that these zones were successful as loggers accepted the payments in lieu of their activities. Our desire to recognise the creation of safe zones as good would hold us back from looking for evidence of other activities. We would have missed the fact that the loggers were rewarded twice: once by not logging in the safe zones, and a second time by moving their continued logging activities outside of them. In the end, the objective is the reduction of greenhouse gas emission and not whether trees are preserved in the safe zones or not.

Nature, a leading science journal, published a collection of papers on the *Challenges in Irreproducible Research* in 2018. This was from a recognition of *mea culpa* arising from a period of introspection in the medical science community. Many published results, which were peer reviewed and checked, had been found to be irreproducible. That is, all the checks and bounds and mathematical reassurances of statistical significance were unable to ensure that there were no biases. What happened was that the whole process was centred around reporting positive results. This created a *hypothesis myopia* that was ultimately damaging to genuine efforts to improve health.

Two papers in the collection were particularly interesting with regards to the investment industry. The first paper is by freelance science writer Regina Nuzzo, who describes how we are masters of self-deception. When we market sustainable investing, we focus on the points we want to make and ignore the evidence that is either against them or is seemingly irrelevant to them. The other paper is about how two research prizes were set up in 2017 to reward negative results. This is crucially important, as we need to demonstrate the falsehood of sustainability thinking as much as to validate its potential veracity. When the investment industry makes any claims about performance, it is obfuscating a fundamental issue: sustainability is not about financial returns.

For the categories of risk mitigation and performance seeking, the information to help with the assessment of the risk and the selection of opportunities comes largely from questionnaires and surveys filled voluntarily by businesses. The goal is to have information from every company in the world. In reality, data from only a few thousand companies is tabulated. It is a work in progress, but with each year, more are added. However, many will never be included, partly because the work involved is onerous for many companies to do. The ones that have had their data tabulated are typically the larger companies.

The data companies behind the ESG data are the ones that construct the questionnaires. They also provide a degree of quality control and will respond to the users if there are issues identified. The data points themselves are split into the three categories of environmental, social, and governance. The environmental aspects cover areas of emission, technological and product innovation, and resource use. Each of these is further subdivided into sub-categories, with a number of data points associated with each sub-category. In a similar way, the social aspects are concerned with areas of workforce, data privacy, human rights, and charity involvements. For the governance aspects, the focus is on how the company is run and covers management structure, diversity, shareholder communications and voting procedures, as well as corporate responsibility. Sustainability reporting is generally included as a governance matter, typically in the form of whether there is a sustainability policy or not, and what the reporting hierarchy for sustainability efforts is.

A typical business is faced with hundreds, if not thousands of questions from each of the ESG data providers. When looked at in this way, it is not surprising that there is a systematic bias in favour of the larger multi-national companies. They can afford to dedicate staff and research to ensure they score well. Another bias we found was that companies that have diverse businesses do better, even if some of these businesses are in recognisably harmful areas. This is because an empty response carries a negative score to mitigate the situation where a company avoids answering questions in areas where it is doing poorly. The result is the more responses that are given, the better. Smaller more focused companies, therefore, find themselves at a disadvantage.

As a demonstration of the kind of bias the data may have, we found in one of these datasets the worst scoring businesses were a number of small renewable energy companies. Digging deeper, we found this was because they did not have the resources to report across the breadth of the questionnaire.

There are always issues with data. With time, much of these deficiencies will no doubt be improved. However, the one thing they point to which will not change is that recording how a business operates does not equate to how sustainable our world will be. As long as sustainable investing considers these two things as equal, then Ellen Hanak's comment which we quoted in reference to California's sustainable groundwater plans will apply. Namely, we will all be thinking we are doing the right thing but together the problem will continue and worsen. Sustainable investing has to consider not only if there are limits to growth, but whether there are also limits to investments.

The ESG data companies sell their data to fund managers, typically charging according to the size of the asset under management. The amount of work needed to be done does not depend on the size of the assets, but this is a way for them to gain more profit if there is more money coming into this space. It emphasises an agency problem inherent in the investment industry. The more assets the industry manages, the more it will be paid, even when the effort is no different for $10 billion or $100 billion of investments. This makes all the people involved focus on growth and is a fundamental issue as growth itself is the source of the problem.

When we consider the risks to sustainability, the biggest risk is simply too much money being deployed for the purpose of profits. This presents an obvious dilemma as the industry and the data providers are all vested to promote growth, and regulators and policymakers are also keen on increasing the amount of money involved. As the size of investments increases, genuine opportunities become scarce, and profits become more important to drive the momentum. We see sustainable stock market indices outperforming traditional indices, and this has happened not because they have realised a reduction in the global temperatures, but because we are willing to pay upfront in the hope that we are doing something right. As profits increase, we simply draw more people who are interested in profits into the area and turn sustainable investments further into pure marketing devices.

True sustainability requires a more patient approach. If the objective is a reduction in global temperatures, significant profits should only come when this is achieved. We have the situation now where new ventures are effectively funded for free. Pension funds and other investment funds are more interested in giving good sounding annual reports on their sustainability efforts than in developing a proper and scientific understanding of how to contain the aggregate damages from investments. If we are serious about sustainable investing, we need to ask why we are seeing higher sustainable investment returns when global temperatures are still rising.

As for the investment process itself, each manager will have their own way of incorporating this data. The following will give a sense of how it works in general. Suppose our aim is to select companies across a range of industries to create a portfolio that has good prospects of financial performance and also has reasonable ESG practices. We can start by setting a minimum ESG score as a threshold for a company to qualify for potential selection. Within this subset of companies, the ones with the best anticipated performance can then be identified.

The approach of going for the best score reflects the current trend in thinking that the way to sustainability is only to invest in those companies which are deemed currently as sustainable. There are problems with this. The first is again that a high ESG score cannot be equated with a sustainable outcome. It could just as equally mean a worse outcome in terms of physical sustainability. The converse of this is equally true. Low ESG scores do not necessarily mean that those businesses may not contribute beneficially to the potential physical outcomes.

A second problem is counter-intuitive to our current push to divest from fossil fuel investments. If we want to stop fossil fuels from being used, then we need to own the fossil fuels so that we can control whether they are extracted or not. That means owning the companies that own the oil fields like Shell and BP, for example, even if that taints our sustainability credentials. The high score approach encourages us to sell out of our ownership of these companies. Morally, this is washing our hands of the responsibility. The risk mitigation aspect of sustainable investing encourages divesting because it limits the potential losses to our portfolios. The other category of performance seeking investing also encourages us to divest from them.

However, sustainability is not about our portfolios. Sustainability choices cannot be made on a profit basis and responsibility has costs. If an investment causes harm but provides us with profits, then if we are genuine in wanting to stop the activities that are causing the harm, it has to cost us those profits. Anything which does not do so is only possible if someone else is continuing the harm and is sharing the profits with us. That is what divesting means. Our hands may look clean and smell fresh, but we are complicit. When we sell our shares in these companies they will go into private hands who care less about the impact.

This ownership model to take special assets off the market is what organisations like the World Land Trust are doing in the areas of nature conservation. The trust has among its patrons the natural history documentary guru, Sir David Attenborough. It buys up land essential to endangered species to remove it from the possibility of being exploited. The irony with fossil fuel is we already own most of it. We are so desperate to wash our hands of it when, as owners, we could be working out how to keep it in the ground. In the end, we will likely repurchase what we are selling now as we realise the mistakes we are making, and give further profits to profiteers who will then demand a much higher price to sell back to us.

Fossil fuel companies also control the whole chain of production, and by being owners we can make the call on how much of the fossil fuels can be extracted, to whom it can be sold and at what price. Even as we worry about the carbon emission from them, fossil fuels will remain important for a good while yet. Through our ownership, we can target how they can be used to benefit those who need them most. This way we are more likely to have a beneficial influence.

As owners, we can also direct research into ways in which the assets may be used without emitting greenhouse gases. It is possible to recapture the greenhouse gases by modifying the process in which the energy is extracted from them to emit only water vapour, and use alternative chemical pathways which do not produce carbon dioxide at all.

The issue is fundamentally an issue of governance. Currently, the G in ESG is not about creating a proper democratic representation of ownership. It is simply about monitoring the management teams to ensure they are not excessive in unethical behaviour, and about following social responsibility values that are defined for us by supranational agencies, like the UN. If we owned a company that has a tremendous reserve of fossil fuel, we should be able to direct research into areas that we think are worth pursuing.

This kind of representation is considered beyond the ability of small shareholders to decide. There is a fair degree of management arrogance to this. It ignores the fact, for example, that Albert Einstein was a small shareholder through TIAA-CREF, and his knowledge might just have been that little bit more extensive on some of these scientific matters than members of the management boards at his time.

Going for the best sustainability score also embeds a potentially dangerous incentive. Because a company with a high ESG data score will have a better chance of being selected into portfolios, and therefore of being valued more highly, it will have a better financial performance. This encourages management boards to look to their ESG scores for financial reasons. The result is what we have been seeing, sustainable investments have performed very well. The dangerous result is it gives the scores a financial incentive, and this displaces the focus from achieving actual sustainability to attaining financial rewards.

Regulators are aware of this issue, as are many of the investment firms. From the regulators' perspectives, the European Union is the most forward thinking in advocating a comprehensive standard of measurements and thresholds that is linked to the physical limits for each of the elements in our industrial and business service processes. By establishing a standard for reporting, it hopes to regulate businesses in terms of the actual quantity of damage done.

This standard is known as the *EU taxonomy for Sustainable Activities*; it will be possible to regulate businesses to limit the individual levels of damage. As an example of the levels of details this taxonomy covers, the following is a randomly selected extract:

> Thresholds for cement Clinker (A) are applicable to plants that produce clinker only, and do not produce finished cement. All other plants need to meet the thresholds for cement or alternative binder (A) Cement clinker: Specific emissions (calculated according to the methodology used for EUETS benchmarks) associated to the clinker production processes are lower than the value of the related EU-ETS benchmark. As of February 2020, the EU-ETS benchmark value for cement clinker manufacturing is: 0.766 tCO2e/t of clinker (B) Cement: Specific emissions associated to the clinker and cement production processes are lower than: 0.498 tCO2e/t of cement or alternative binder.

Clinker is stony residue in cement production, formed by heating the raw materials together at a high temperature to transform them chemically and physically. The clinker provides the bonding property needed, and is mixed with other materials to make the final product. The numbers indicate the amount of carbon emission that is permitted.

This taxonomy is still new, and we do not yet know how it will be incorporated into legislation. While it hopes to set limits for each company, it is the total activity that matters. Not only is regulating the total difficult, but when you have more companies involved that present themselves as sustainable, competition generally leads to growth in the whole market. So instead of 10 companies each producing two units of harm each, we may end up with 100 companies each producing one unit of harm, and each company believing that they are operating sensibly and sustainably, even as the total harm has increased fivefold. Operating more 'sustainably' to prescribed formulas can lull us into becoming more unsustainable.

As for the governance aspect, both the setup with regards to the way companies can involve small shareholders and the way collective investment pools allow the wishes of the investors to be expressed are outdated. The result is that when we invest through collective investment pools, the investment manager ends up with unilateral authority to decide for us. This is done without any proper solicitation of our views. Generally, proper representation is considered simply as somewhere between too complex for the investor to understand and too expensive to do. The management teams of companies also generally prefer independence from shareholders, especially small shareholders. The result is that there is really no ability for us to have our say.

Some of us may, for example, prefer the companies we invest in to pay more contributions to our public services through taxation and accept a lower return from them. Others may prefer them to be even more aggressive at tax avoidance. If we are all owners of the same company by virtue of our shareholdings, then there should be a platform where such views can achieve representation. Companies will need to experiment with different ways of governance to improve how these wishes can be expressed. We are ultimately the true owners of the companies; the investment managers and the management teams of the companies work for us. In the end, however, the same company cannot be both aggressive at tax avoidance and be obliging in its tax position.

What tends to happen is that activist movements either in the form of social and environmental justice groups or in the form of activist shareholders end up setting the agenda. Social and environmental justice groups tend to focus on topical issues and express this through lobbying and vocal action. Activist shareholders tend to focus on profits and tend to do this by becoming a significant minority shareholder to influence the company's controlling board of directors. Neither approach addresses the fundamental issue of why we need to invest, and unless we can resolve the needs that drive us to invest, investments will always target the highest possible returns.

If we prefer a high street with friendly shops, proper governance should allow us to control the companies we own so that the small shops are not destroyed. If we consider that being in a community with people we recognise is important, we should ensure our companies recognise this as something to preserve. When we look to our future and consider our retirement, if we are not to rely purely on a pool of money, then it is highly likely that we will need to continue working. We may therefore want to direct the companies we own to provide employment opportunities for us as we age, and ensure our experience and knowledge are used so that we can work constructively with the younger generations without being in competition with them.

Sustainable investing could look at governance to make fundamental changes, but it is unlikely to happen because of the vested interests embedded in the investment industry.

The investment tracking service, *Morningstar*, has been monitoring investor flows into sustainable investing. It reported a record inflow of $54.6bn for the second quarter of 2020, with hundreds of new funds launched in that quarter. This flow reflects our wish to do good. The companies that answer the surveys and the data companies that compile their answers all try to provide a constructive picture of what may help us to build a better planet. We also have our part to do. The most fundamental aspect of that is to recognise that our investments can do great harm.

One comment we found in our research is worth repeating. Matthew Kiernan, a veteran of ESG investments who authored a book on the subject in 2007, raised a question: "What's wrong with leaving some money on the table and avoid doing what may clearly be the wrong thing?"

Q&A

Q: Given there are so many things going on, and they are all linked together, we can talk till the cows come home, whether it is the fault of the super-rich, fossil fuels, financialisation, short-termism in business, wealth inequality, or just our own greed. Is there anything we should absolutely stop doing?

A: We must stop believing that we don't need sacrifices or that individual actions don't matter.

What we do does matter because we influence others.

We have responsibility for what's going on. Our economic system is meant to serve us, and we have to take control of it. We do this by stopping ourselves from giving in to it. This means we will have to accept some costs, and we must be honest about our reasons and be open to talking about them. This way, what we do can influence others and allow ethics to emerge.

CHAPTER 10:

CHOICES

Face your fears and don't play the game.
It is rigged.

How much do you have for your retirement and is that amount enough?

The median UK annual full-time salary is £31,467. This means 12 million of the UK's 24 million full-time workers earn less than this amount a year, and the other half earns more. If we simplify the numbers and imagine you worked for 30 years earning £30,000 a year, your total lifetime earnings would be £900,000. The current legislation in the UK requires 8% of salary to be paid as pension contributions towards retirement. As 8% of £900,000 is £72,000, this is the size of the pension pot you may draw on if you did not have any investment gains. This pot needs to last for 20 or more years.

If you earn 60% or less of what half of the working population is earning, then you are considered to be in poverty. Since half of the population earns less than £31,467 per year, 60% of this amount is a tad over £18,000 per year. So if you want to stay ahead of the poverty level of income in retirement, your pension will need to provide you with at least £18,000 a year for 20 plus years. This is clearly not possible just with the £72,000 saved.

Most people do not imagine being below the poverty level in their retirement. They do not know either how large their pension pot needs to be. What they can work out is that if they live for 20 years in retirement, and each year needs £18,000, that is a total of £360,000 needed. This is about five times the £72,000 they would have saved. So to achieve a pot of £360,000, the money they save needs to produce a 10% growth each year and for every year throughout the years that they are saving. This 10% is incidentally the level of returns we are expecting, according to the Schroder's investor survey that we pointed to earlier. This amount of growth is also what we have expressed as not possible without either forcing ourselves and others to be poorer while we work, or by exploiting our planet in ways we may not wish to, or both.

Even though the reality is that we may not need quite as much for our final savings pot, as we may be able to live on less and have some other means of income in retirement, we are still basically left with a 'Hobson's choice'. That is, no choice except to grow our savings by as much as possible.

Too much money chasing high returns is a bad thing, so this choice is a bad thing. However, to turn away from following this choice is difficult. We cannot just stop what we are doing. All we can do is tinker around the edges. To do more than that requires a fundamental rethinking of how we individually want to face our future and will carry significant personal costs.

Thomas Hobson who is credited with the phrase 'Hobson's choice' was the University Carrier at Cambridge in England. His job was to carry post on horseback between Cambridge and London in the 16th century. Through his entrepreneurial activities, he became one of the wealthiest men in Cambridge, and the town still has several streets bearing his name. Hobson's Conduit, for example, is a gully running alongside the main roads leading to the city centre. The construction for it was started in 1610 to bring water to the city at a time when the existing supply was thought to have been responsible for several outbreaks of the plague. Thomas Hobson funded the project and established a trust for its upkeep which has continued to this day. At his death, John Milton, the poet known for *Paradise Lost*, was a student at the university and contributed several poems about his life. The phrase 'Hobson's choice' comes from his business practice and its origin is explained in a letter to *The Spectator* magazine in 1712:

> Mr. Tobias [sic] Hobson, from whom we have the Expression, was a very honourable Man, for I shall ever call the Man so who gets an Estate honestly. Mr. Tobias Hobson was a Carrier, and being a Man of great Abilities and Invention, and one that saw where there might good Profit arise, though the duller Men overlooked it; this ingenious Man was the first in this Island who let out Hackney-Horses. He lived in Cambridge, and observing that the Scholars rid hard, his manner was to keep a large Stable of Horses, with Boots, Bridles, and Whips to furnish the Gentlemen at once, without going from College to College to borrow, as they have done since the Death of this worthy Man: I say, Mr. Hobson kept a Stable of forty good Cattle, always ready and fit for travelling; but when a Man came for a Horse, he was led into the Stable, where there was great Choice, but he obliged him to take the Horse which stood next to the Stable-Door; so that every Customer was alike well served according to his Chance, and every Horse ridden with the same Justice: From whence it became a Proverb, when what ought to be your Election was forced upon you, to say, Hobson's Choice.

The same phrase, *Hobson's Choice*, was used by Harold Brighouse as the title of a play. Written in 1916 and set in Salford near Manchester in England in 1880, the play depicted the transformation of a well-to-do widower named Henry Hobson, who was father to three daughters. The play has been highly successful. It was first put on in New York and is frequently performed since. It was made into a silent movie in 1920, adapted for TV, made into a Broadway musical, and performed even as a ballet. It is perhaps best known for the 1954 film version which featured Charles Laughton as the father.

The play and the film depict the lives of the father and his daughters with money and negotiations featuring prominently. The economics of the situations play a central role in determining the choices of all the characters and dictates their actions; they all have no choice but to comply.

The eldest of the daughters, Maggie, is competent and driven. Through her actions, economic efficiency is achieved and as this happens, it brings about benefits that allow the characters to establish their own futures. However, as the play progresses, the characters become increasingly beholden to the economics of their situations and lose their choices.

The transformation starts with Maggie herself. Her sisters have suitors, but her father does not want Maggie to marry because his business will be lost without her. Her services come for free. Faced with the prospect of being nothing more than "a proper old maid", Maggie sees that her only choice lies in a "business idea in the shape of a man". Willie Mossop is a skilled but mentally stunted workman. Maggie seizes on this, forcing Willie's girlfriend to admit that his economic prospects will be better with Maggie and to give him up. Together the couple try to negotiate better employment terms with the father, who refuses and threatens them with violence. The couple end up with no choice but to start their own business.

In the 1954 film version, Maggie convinces a wealthy client who particularly likes Willie's work to lend £100 at 20% interest for one year and uses the money to establish a basement in Oldfield

Road as their shop, workshop and living space. As the business progresses, Maggie gains control of her life. She is able to negotiate marriage settlements for her sisters to marry into money and class, in return for accepting her own marriage to Willie even though he is just a workman. The settlements allow them to marry, and so they comply.

By the end of the play, Willie is fully transformed from being the mentally stunted workman to being the proprietor of both his own business and Henry Hobson's business. Maggie herself is forced to accept the reversal of roles, in recognition that Willie now controls the economics and therefore controls the situation. She accepts this symbolically by agreeing to his name headlining the new business: 'Mossop and Hobson'.

In the case of Thomas Hobson, he was the agent who determined which horse was to be nearest to the door and therefore controlled the client's choice. In Harold Brighouse's play, economic process is the agent of choice, and even though everyone benefits economically, they all forfeit their freedoms. For us, today, our choices are also Hobson's choices. We are offered plenty of alternatives but they are all dictated by an economic system that focuses singularly on growth. All our choices are towards growth.

For most of us, our workday is a repetition of getting up early and hurrying through morning rituals so that we can be in time for our commutes to work. Those of us who are fortunate enough to live close to our workplace may avoid jostling with the many others who are commuting by mass transit like ourselves. By and large, we are herded and funnelled to our workplaces. The stations see hundreds of thousands of us passing through, all mostly during the same short hours.

We focus our thoughts on not disturbing others and not to be disturbed ourselves. The day comes as a series of chores, whether we enjoy them or not is irrelevant. There are meetings we need to attend and calls we need to make. These are interspersed with emails we need to send or to answer. Increasingly, we spend more and more time in front of screens. We do our tasks. We also spend as much if not more time reporting on what we have done. Our day is measured and monitored with the purpose of making it more efficient. When the day finishes, we reverse our commutes, sometimes pausing to catch a drink with friends.

We do this because our economic system divides the work that is needed into little units and we each take a share and implicitly follow the set paths. We readily comply with it and give up our choices along the way because, like the characters in Brighouse's play, we rely on the benefits of being in this system.

In this world, it is economic progress that determines choices. The pattern of our lives is set by what improves productivity. We are like the customers in Henry Ford's remark on his famous Model T automobile: "Any customer can have a car painted any colour that he wants so long as it is black." The reason was that the Model T was the most profitable model, and it happened to have been black. We are offered our choices because they are the ones that generate the most profits.

The meetings and planning in our work are all organised to help us deliver better profits. Since what is one person's leisure is another's work, our rest moments too are subtly shaped into producing better profits. We may see ourselves as simply having a cup of coffee or taking a spa day, but these activities are the measured economic outputs of someone else.

Our inventiveness goes into solving the problems we meet along the way so that we can sustain this drive for profits and strengthen the continuance of this economic progress. Nothing stops it, and nothing escapes it. The economic system shapes our choices from the moment of conception through the choices offered to our parents. They become choices over the schools we attend and the lessons we take. The choices determine the social groups we mix with and the universities we apply to. These steps lead to the careers we follow. Family, love, work, and retirement are all shaped into efficient units that slot into one other. It is economic progress that allows for better welfare for everyone.

It is, as a taxi driver said once in a conversation in London, "They make the hours so long that you don't have time to think about how wrong it is."

Although the model has been powerful and hugely successful, there have always been ideological objections. There were the counter-culture movements in the '60s and satirical comedies like *The Good Life* in the UK in the '70s. The Green Party movement and the Occupy movement which followed the Global Financial Crisis all protested against it. The current Extinction Rebellion is also objecting to this economic system. However, our inventiveness and adaptability ultimately absorb all these objections in our marketing. The objections themselves, such as the current ideology for all things ethical, social, and green, simply become yet another way to continue our growth. We recognise our wish to be green, for example, and choose green products. These products do well and generate a different consumption, but still a consumption, and create more profits. We wish to be more socially aware, so we demand more corporate social responsibility. The companies comply and offer us labelled goods so we can shop freely with our consciences clear. We buy more, supporting the companies to grow, and create more profits.

The result is that there is very little choice in our lives. Choices are there only to help us believe that we are free to choose, much like the magician when he asks us to pick a card. The card is forced and we will pick the one he wishes; the other cards are there to make us feel there is magic. We can choose from one thing or another, but all the choices lead to the same thing – growth.

The system has become one where we cannot allow it to stop. It has become a knot of such complexity that there is no way to unravel it. Everything is linked to everything else. If we take something like work, we will find that work is not simply about what we do in our jobs. Work is about housing and health, and probably a good number of other things unrelated to what we do in our jobs.

A 2018 survey commissioned by Together, a specialist lender in the United Kingdom, found that 54% of mortgage applicants were denied a loan for no other reason than being self-employed or being on contract work. Full-time work makes a difference because our economic system links mortgage qualification to it. If you are self-employed, you typically need a year's income record before you can be assessed for your creditworthiness. If you have a full-time job, it does not matter if the job only started one week ago, you are immediately eligible for assessment.

In the US, health insurance is an issue for people who are not in full-time work. To have your work provide health insurance is a nice benefit. However, company-sponsored health insurance is the largest tax exclusion item in the US budget. As the premium is tax-deductible, the companies have little incentive to drive the premium levels lower. The cost of health insurance therefore becomes so high that individuals cannot afford it. Getting a job is therefore about getting access to healthcare.

All these interconnections have been fine because we have all benefitted individually, and in aggregate society is genuinely better off. The problem comes when we start pushing up against social and planetary boundaries. Unlike the Gold Rush era where there were vast and pristine areas of our planet available to exploit and economic migration of people was largely a non-issue, the choice to seek the highest economic growth in our current context can only push us through those boundaries and to our individual and collective detriment. It is like the march of soldiers on a bridge. When there are only a few soldiers, there is plenty of room on the bridge and the force of their footsteps is not significant. It matters not if they march in sync or not, but when the whole battalion crosses and marches to the same tune, the bridge breaks.

There have been considerable efforts made to reduce our footprint on the planet. Green initiatives dominate everywhere. Every government has a carbon net-zero policy, and every company advertises its green, social, and diversity action plans. We have looked into many of these. They all give the impression that there are no issues anymore. Their intentions are genuine and their statements are backed by scientific authorities. However, no company has yet asked us to buy less of their products or stated that they need to reduce their profits, and no government has stood for election on a policy of deliberately slowing down our economic growth. They all offer us their promises to deliver either a world where resources are infinite and our growth will never breach any boundaries, or one where growth can continue without using any new resources. This is simply the way in which our economic system transforms our intentions into a single choice, which is to grow further.

We are all driven to serve our own self-interest. Attempting to act differently raises the fear in us of going down an irreversible path towards destitution for ourselves and our families. This prompts us to prepare for the worst case. A study in 2018 in Miami-Dade County, Florida, suggests 'climate gentrification' is happening. Property prices are rising faster for houses in more elevated locations above sea level. Through the way in which our economic system connects work, education, housing, leisure, health and other things, this gentrification drags along with it greater social inequalities and diminishes the social diversity that we will likely need to deal with climate change.

When resources become scarce, an economic system that allows us to act in our own self-interest changes from being positive-sum, where everyone gets to benefit, to becoming zero-sum, where for every winner there has to be a loser. We have turned a collective drive for growth into a race for growth, where we will only reap benefits if we are the ones who win the race. It is a classic prisoner's dilemma. This is a situation where two people are connected by a common event, a crime they committed together, and they have the option of either putting their own self-interest first or trusting each other. In the former case, the prisoner who tells on the other first can negotiate for a lighter sentence. In the latter case, when they both trust each other and remain silent, there is no evidence to convict either of them. In a finite world, we are all connected by our use of resources, but this makes us all feel pressured to stay ahead of others no matter where we find ourselves in the wealth distribution.

In November 2020, the actress Lori Loughlin started serving a prison sentence. She was found guilty of having illegally paid to get her daughters a place at the University of Southern California. Operation Varsity Blues was the name given for the FBI investigation into bribery and cheating for admission into prestigious US universities, and it led to the arrests and charges against many high-profile and wealthy parents. There has been much written on the subject to provide celebrity drama, much gloating over how terrible these people are with all their wealth and privileges, using it to demonstrate the corruption of entitlement.

More seriously, some of these articles brought up earlier cases of families at the opposite end of the income distribution. Kelley Williams-Bolar was convicted for using her father's address to get her daughters into a better performing school. Homeless Tanya McDowell was charged with larceny for stealing $15,000, the cost of her son's public education, after using her babysitter's address to enrol him, and was sentenced to jail. In the process and as a bizarre demonstration of justice, the babysitter was evicted from her home.

The real question, however, is why do even rich people feel the pressure to act like this for a university place? We can understand Tanya McDowell and Kelley Williams-Bolar for wanting better schooling for their children since education is the best way for them to advance from their poverty. The culprits of Operation Varsity Blues were, however, people who were well-off. The fact that they were caught and convicted suggests that even for them, the pressures to get into these universities are real.

Attending a top-ranking university has come to mean much more than being educated by the best recognised academic minds in their particular fields. If it were only that there would be much less pressure. In fact, two students at Stanford University, Erica Olsen and Kalea Woods, brought a class action suit in the aftermath of Operation Varsity Blues against their university which confirmed that attending these colleges is not about education.

Learning did not feature at all in their suit. In their submission, they claim, "Acceptance of a student into one of these universities often makes it easier for a student to obtain a high-paying job or career after graduation." The damage being claimed, aside from the auxiliary issue of the application fees, is "her degree is now not worth as much as it was before, because prospective employers may now question whether she was admitted to the university on her own merits, versus having parents who were willing to bribe school officials." It matters not how well you do at Stanford, it matters only that you were accepted into Stanford.

The BBC reported in 2019 the results of a survey. It showed that graduates of the 24 top UK universities, otherwise known as the Russell Group universities, are more likely to find work soon after graduation. Some of this, undoubtedly, is due to the fact that the top universities cream off the better students; therefore we cannot tell if the survey results are showing that the top 24 universities are better at selecting the candidates who are more likely to find a job soon after graduation; that being accepted at one of the top universities actually improves the chances of finding a job soon after graduation; or, as it perhaps should be, the education is better and employers value the wisdom and knowledge gained. Certainly, Olsen and Woods's point is that being accepted by them is what counts, not what is studied there.

Then again, one comment to the BBC article points to a different sentiment: "Given the quality of most of our politicians and the fact that most of them went to the Oxbridge universities... they must be the worst universities in the country." This, however, only serves to emphasise it is the name of the university that matters and not what happens there.

Employers, to their credit, are quick to point out they have name-blind policies. A UK Department of Business Innovation & Skills study on *Understanding employers' graduate recruitment and selection practices* surveyed 84 institutions, and found:

> The interviews with employers uncovered fairly limited evidence that indicated employers targeted solely elite/high-entry tariff universities in their attraction strategies or in their selection practices; or viewed them as necessarily producing the most able students. This was at odds with the views of several stakeholders, who felt a degree from a Russell Group university was important in order to access some of the [top] graduate programmes.

In the end though, no matter what people may say, it matters which university you attend. It matters not necessarily because the employers think it matters; it matters because people think employers think it matters. This is embedded into the choices, or rather the lack of choices, offered by our economic system.

A 2017 report by the United Kingdom's Department for Education showed that houses within catchment areas of primary schools which are ranked in the top decile for their performances were 38.8% more expensive in London than the average house price in the same locality. In the North East of the country where house prices were lowest, the prices for houses near the top decile schools were still at a premium of 10.4% above the average. Whether a family is living in the less expensive North East, with an average house price of £129,800, or the more expensive London where the average house price was £484,700, access to good education is crystallised into a differential in house prices.

A family in the North East is forced to come up with an extra £13,500, or 10.4% of the average house price, to be near to their top schools. They may think that this extra £13,500 would be easy for a London family that can afford £484,700 for a house to come up with. In reality, the London family needs an additional £190,000 to be near to their top schools. This is a premium that is almost four times as large in percentage terms and more than 14 times as large in monetary terms than that of the family in the North East. Regardless of whether we are rich or not, we are all under the same pressure, and if we are to respond to it we will have no choice but to choose more growth and more profits.

Our social psychology is important to how we perceive and respond to these pressures. When Richard and I were discussing this with friends, one of them pointed us to Alfred Adler. Whereas Maslow's hierarchy of needs highlighted our innate psychological driver to motivations, Adler, in his book *Social Interest: A Challenge to Mankind,* describes how the context of social expectations determine how we see ourselves in "the problems of communal life, of work, and of love". Our social awareness commences from early childhood and ultimately means we end up viewing society's appreciation of our worth through the payments we receive. Pay, therefore, is not just about money and what we can do with it; it is about how we see others and how others see us. The satirist HL Mencken said it best more than a century ago, wealth is any "income that is at least $100 more a year than the income of one's wife's sister's husband". Our very sense of worth is locked into the social hierarchies of the economy.

Social psychologists at the University of North Carolina confirmed this in a study in 2014, and they further noted that when people merely perceived themselves as having moved to a higher social status, regardless of whether in reality they had or not, they shifted their fundamental beliefs. Importantly, this happened while they still believed that their views had not changed. If we think we have progressed economically, we will believe the social system is fair, even if prior to this progression we had felt it was unfair. So, as soon as we feel we might be getting ahead, we prefer the system in the way it is. Once again, because we perceive it in this way, that same economic structure is reinforced and persisted.

To be $100 ahead of your wife's brother-in-law is to engage in a perpetual chase with him, and the chase generates consumption along the way. It matters not if this consumption happens in a conventional manner or in green and socially equitable manners; once the chase is set, the outcome is the same in all cases. Namely, it is a continued push for growth.

Marketing subtly takes on the challenge to promote this chase, introducing us to all the products that help us to feel and demonstrate we have that $100 more. As this chase progresses, it further demands that we consume the $100. The higher paying job is met through social expectations with higher living costs. Our services cost more, and we frequent shops which are more expensive. Our work takes up more of our time, and so our holiday times become more restricted and our holidays are more expensive. Gradually, everything costs more. When our hypothetical wife's brother-in-law catches up, or we fear that he may be doing so, consciously or not we push on again.

In the light of all of this, if we cannot keep up, we cheat. The same report that showed the premium in the house prices around schools that have been recognised as higher performing also tabulated the strategies parents used to gain an advantage for their offspring's education. We may employ private tutors, attend church services so that our child could enter a more reputable church school, or use our relatives' addresses. Those in social group A representing the better off and therefore likely to have greater resources employ all the strategies listed. Those in groups D and E with fewer resources tend to rely on relatives' addresses and church attendance.

This cheating is actually good for our economic growth, and so, we socialise it. Employing tutors, attending church services, buying second homes, moving houses to different catchment areas, or making school appeals: these strategies all generate more activities. People get jobs and have more work as a result. Ultimately, they translate into more growth. All this feeds into better returns for our savings and investments. In reality, we do not frown upon cheating, we accept it with its benefits without too much questioning.

The practices extend far beyond schools. Companies that cannot improve on their real productivity generate the semblance of growth through share buybacks. This is done either with real cash from revenues that they are not trying to reinvest, or in the worst cases, they finance this by borrowing money. By buying its own shares in the open market, a company causes its share price to move up and signals that it is a company that is worth purchasing. Others who see this may piggyback on the activity in the hope of making a quick return. The activity does not produce any more real goods, but it does boost returns for our savings and investments.

However, nothing is truly victimless. As with all things economic, there is always some feedback that triggers other consequences. These activities lead investors to believe that high returns are perpetually possible, and companies with ordinary returns are put at a disadvantage. Ultimately, it forces other businesses into competing through bad practices.

Marketing also helps us to cheat. It creates artificial stratifications of products so that no matter which level of wealth we are at, we can still be that $100 ahead. Look up outlet shopping on the internet and you will find plenty of blogs presenting the best of outlet villages, defined as places where 20 or more luxury brands offer discounts of over 25% from normal high street prices in their own shops. These mini towns include places like Bicester Village near London, McArthurGlen Designer Outlet in Malaga, La Vallée Village near Disneyland in Paris with its rural French chic, Torino Outlet Village just outside the city, and the Florentia Villages in China. From a brand perspective, they offer a cheaper channel than traditional instore shopping, with the ability to offload out-of-season items and increasingly specific lines designed for the outlet market.

To create a sense of luxury, especially in today's selfie and the continuously social messaging world, outlet centres have also focused on their architectural appeal. In China, outlet villages are built as classic stereotypes of European villages to cater to those who are not able to travel, and in Europe, iconic architecture is used as a mark of sophistication. The Torino Village, designed by Claudio Silvestrin, for example, is a winner of the 2020 Iconic Awards for Innovative Architecture.

All this comes inevitably back to our investments. Nuveen, the property arm of TIAA-CREF, the American teachers' pension fund that we started this book with our discussion of vineyards, is surprisingly the investor behind the Florentia Villages in China. DWS, the German asset manager for pensions and retail investments, is the investor behind many of Europe's outlet villages. Similarly, other investment managers seeking 'alternatives' to enhance their returns do so by supplying capital to opportunities that are marketed to appeal to our consumption. These play on that sense of being $100 ahead. So our demand for financial returns creates yet another feedback to the physical world, driving marketing that targets our psychological motivators, and our economic system entrenches this as more choice, but only that choice that guides us to a path of growth.

In the end, the problem is the nature of choice. When Hezekiah Thrift wrote that letter to *The Spectator* in 1712, he preceded his description of Hobson's choice with an explanation of it:

> ...by vulgar Errour is taken and used when a Man is reduced to an Extremity, whereas the Propriety of the Maxim is to use it when you would say, there is Plenty, but you must make such a Choice, as not to hurt another who is to come after you.

In the hands of a 'good' person, like Thomas Hobson, as demonstrated by his concern for the City of Cambridge's health which can still be seen today in the waterway that bears his name, the choice was about 'not to hurt another'.

The central issue of choice is this: are we willing to do what we believe may be the right thing even if it means we risk falling behind? If the right thing is 'not to hurt another', then are we willing to leave money on the table and risk not having sufficient funds in our own pension pots to do this? If you speak with an environmental or social justice warrior, it is obvious that the choice exists, and we are irresponsible at best and plain evil at worst if we do not leave money on the table. Greta Thunberg, in her 2019 address to the UN, memorable for her intense glare down at Donald Trump, baited the baby boomer generation in this exact way with being evil:

> You say you hear us and that you understand the urgency, but no matter how sad and angry I am, I do not want to believe that. Because if you really understood the situation and still kept on failing to act then you would be evil...

If by leaving money on the table we expose ourselves and those we care for to unacceptable risks, then we may consider it evil to expose ourselves in this way. So, if leaving money on the table and not leaving money on the table are both evil choices, even if we were to argue they are different kinds of evil, do we really have a choice?

We are like the characters in Brighouse's play, our habits governed by an economic rationale that is set on growth. Within this, we may tinker, but we have no choice.

CHAPTER 11:

GOOD VS EVIL

Good comes not from what we do, but from what we don't do. Start thinking about that.

In the autumn of 1985, I was starting a doctorate in physics. Not for the last time, I was picking up a new subject and even though I had an undergraduate degree, ploughing through the research materials made me realise just how little I knew. I might have had some knowledge and some vocabulary, but I had little real understanding. Results were described in the papers, but I could not explain how they came about, and certainly could not say if the results were or were not important. It all seemed like some mystical practices. I could read the words aloud but be damned if I understood what they meant.

At the time, I was sharing a house with a political philosopher. His bookshelves were full of volumes from authors like Thomas Hobbes to David Hume and more recent works from Richard Dawkins to EO Wilson, and among them, a book titled *After Virtue*. This was published in 1981 and was written by a Scottish moral philosopher, Alasdair MacIntyre. Born in 1929, he was educated and worked in the UK before emigrating to America. He is considered one of the major moral philosophers of our age. *After Virtue* addressed the demise of virtue, using an analogy to a world where the practice and knowledge of science had been long lost.

Followers of science remained, hanging on to fragments of the language in a reconstruction that was meaningless, much as I was feeling then about my own subject.

In that way, the true meaning of virtue in our world today is largely lost, and instead, we use the language of virtue in an inconsistent and somewhat incoherent way. The point of the science analogy, however, is that there was a proper body of knowledge and meaning. It is just that over time as we gave in to accepting economic benefits and gave up on our obligations and responsibilities, we have accepted too many compromises with the consequence that the meaning of words like 'good' and 'evil' have been lost.

In his second book, *Whose Justice, Which Rationality*, MacIntyre recovers the meaning of moral values through a reference to context. Those values of good and evil derive their precise and well-anchored meaning through the context in which they were introduced. As our society changed, the words stayed, but the context has moved on. We, therefore, lose understanding if we insist on using the same words to ascribe values from a bygone age. To recover moral values, we need to understand the context first.

A world where resources may be considered infinite is entirely different from one where resources are not only finite but are also at their limit. Accordingly, the concepts of good and evil appropriate in the former need to be reconsidered and revised if they are to be meaningful in the latter. Although the words may be spelt the same, what they mean is different.

MacIntyre highlighted Thomas Aquinas in *Whose Justice, Which Rationality*. Aquinas was a Christian philosopher whom the current Pope referred to in his encyclical on sustainability. MacIntyre explained that four conditions are needed to test if action is genuinely good in the Thomist view, that is, in accordance with Aquinas's philosophy. These are: is the intention good, has it been implemented well, has it caused or will it lead to harm, and is the outcome and its fundamental nature good. MacIntyre put it as follows:

> Consider in this respect someone who sets out to construct a house for his or her family. The first way in which he or she has to judge their activity good is in respect of the kind of activity it is: its goodness lies in its being good for human beings to live together commodiously in families, and this activity of construction is good as a means directed by that fundamental *inclinatio*. Second, it is insofar as that person only uses land, materials, and labour which are genuinely his or her own to make use of that the action is morally good, by conforming to the primary precept of the natural law not to take what belongs to another, thus ensuring that the house is genuinely the builder's work and the family's possession. Third, the activity is good insofar as no harmful consequences ensue *per accidens*, as for example by excluding someone else's land from sunlight. And fourth, the activity is good insofar as its cause is the relevant kind of goodness in the individual or individuals carrying out the activity, in this case the virtue of justice.

According to Thomas Aquinas, for something to be good, all four conditions need to be satisfied.

Our general economic context is one where the world has infinite resources. In this context, all our activities are generally considered beneficial, because the threshold for an action to be viewed as good is, simply, if any one of the four conditions is met. For example, if we can say our intention for creating cycle lanes is to help people exercise, which is good, then the creation of cycle lanes is a good thing. If we build an outlet shopping village, and we can identify it as providing a better way to consume unsold goods rather than allowing them to go to waste, then the building of the outlet village is good. If we implement an increase in tax without causing distress, because the implementation is good, then the increase is good. Finally, if we exceed the speed limit and no one is immediately hurt by it, then there would be many who would consider the speeding that we have just done as good.

Conversely, in this context of a world with infinite resources, we consider only those actions which fail all four conditions as evil. That is, if we deliberately intend evil, in an action which we implement explicitly in an evil manner, to achieve an outcome that is blatantly evil, and actually causes harm, then and only then would we universally accept what has happened as evil.

For example, if we intended to own all of the lithium rights in the world for selfish gain, and we do so by violently deposing legitimately elected governments, and along the way we deliberately dislocate local communities from their ancestral home and cause social breakdowns, and achieve a crisis of global shortage of the mineral, only then would we consider this action as evil. However, if we were to present the wanting of the lithium rights as motivated by a purpose of mitigating climate change, then many would accept this reason alone as sufficient to justify all subsequent actions and would support it as something good.

In a world with infinite resources, any harm which may be done will eventually be resolved by growth. In this context, therefore, any action is good as it allows us to do more. It is much easier to permit an activity if someone finds it useful, and not to have to be concerned whether it is universally considered as useful or not. Thus, we only need one of the Thomist conditions for good to be true. This leads to the rationalisations that one man's good is another's evil, or what is one man's meat is another's poison. As long as we can argue someone may eventually benefit, then who is to say that it should be forbidden?

We individually may baulk at permitting this. At some level, it grates against our gut feeling of what is right and wrong. Profligate wastefulness is still something that triggers a bad taste. However, most of us are cautious to admit that we are hardly in the position to condemn others to a loss of their jobs, or to hold them back from the chances of a job; so we accept our economic system to function the way it does.

The issue is actually deeper than this. We always need a system that allows for activities that we do not feel right about. This, in essence, is because no single person or institution can formulate policies that will always serve the good of every individual, in every situation, and at all times. When a factory is created, some land is taken away; when healthcare is extended, someone will pay less attention to their own health. Whatever the activity, to every good we can think of, there will, at some point, be a complement which is evil. We need someone to be the bogeyman, and that is the economic system.

Take the case of the plan for a new coal mine in Cumbria, in the UK. This was approved in 2019 even as the region and the country were planning ambitiously for their carbon net-zero targets. The plan, made by West Cumbria Mining, aims to provide metallurgical coke to the steel industry in the UK and Europe, and in doing so to alleviate the need to import 52 million tonnes of coal a year from the US, Australia, and Russia. In a report by the Executive Director for Economy and Infrastructure, the cases for and against the plan are listed in substantial detail.

The climate change concerns include noting that more coal production means more coal availability, which will ultimately lead to more carbon dioxide. Countering this, the report also lists the benefits that the project will provide, with reassurances of at least 500 jobs, most of which will be filled locally. It will also implement an environmental programme that includes strengthening the local ecology. In the end, planning permission was granted by a unanimous vote and it was ratified by another unanimous vote. Climate activists have, as would be expected, been pushing for intervention to revoke the decision.

The decision anchored on what could be known for certain, such as the provision of the jobs, versus what may be, such as the possible increase in carbon dioxide emissions. We actually feel that coal is better left in the ground. However, the takeaway is that any decision-making system necessarily becomes a bogeyman. If the decision was to refuse to grant the planning permission, then others in favour of the plan would object in an equally vocal way. The harm done to them by a rejection would be felt as equally real.

The economic system which we frequently lambast is deserving of many criticisms, but equally, it serves us so that we can have decisions that we do not wish to make ourselves to be made on our behalf. It keeps our hands clean and keeps us free of guilt. Changing the system will not alter this. When we seek a zero-growth, happiness-driven, doughnut or circular, capitalist or libertarian, socialist or communist economies, whatever the colour, we will still face choices that will seem good to some and evil to others. Even if no decisions were ever to be made, the indecision itself will result in both good and evil.

This does not mean we should keep our views to ourselves. Indeed, it means we should, more than ever, make known what we think are the right choices, as the advocates for both sides in the Cumbria planning consultations have done. It does mean, though, we should not ever expect any economic system to be moral, or to think that if we were able to make it moral, somehow, then all our problems would be solved. If it were a perfect system and decided in favour of climate change on all issues, as we may wish it to do, much harm would still come about to people and communities. When it is perfect, it can only be perfect for one particular group. These decisions will be blatantly evil to others.

This is not just ideological. It is not that we do not agree on what is good and what is evil. Even if we can all agree on what is good and what is evil, there will still be outcomes of good actions that can be significantly harmful to some people. We can all agree that food is good, but some people will become diabetic.

Reinhold Niebuhr takes the idea of a perfect solution further, to say that it is always dangerous, if not outright immoral to pursue it. Niebuhr was an influential 20th century theologian and philosopher. In his book *Moral Man and Immoral Society* he noted that our tendencies to good and to evil may help the individual to become moral, and to act morally; in a group setting, self-serving interests will always win out. So while we, as individuals, may become good because our tendency to good may dominate over our tendency to evil, groups and societies will inevitably and will always become immoral.

Having lived through the Second World War, Niebuhr had no illusions about the evils that groups can do, and undoubtedly his personal experiences shaped his thinking. He saw the extent to which groups can legitimise horrendous actions, genocides even, into moral crusades. His influence in modern politics is substantial. His call for caution in the *Vengence of Victors* has influenced and continues to influence the political discourse. The then President-elect Joe Biden's 2020 post-election speeches reflected this call for caution. Barack Obama held Niebuhr in high esteem, describing him in an interview during his presidential campaign with, "I love him. He's one of my favourite philosophers." To Niebuhr, our tendencies ultimately reveal themselves in a group setting as fanaticism.

A group forms because there is a common interest, and to maintain the group, this needs to be brought to the forefront as a point of identity. Otherwise, the group loses its focus and cohesion, and ceases to be one. When you bring beliefs to the forefront in this way, it creates a point of self-serving interest for the group to maintain cohesion. Individuals, away from the group, diffuse this; they offer independent, rational reasoning when the group becomes locked into groupthink. Martin Luther King Jr referred to Niebuhr in his *Letter from a Birmingham Jail* to explain why individual actions are important.

For sustainability, Niebuhr's understanding matches our scepticism towards the ability of the sustainability movements to achieve their aim without causing more damage. The basic intentions of many of these movements are good, but movements easily turn into fanaticism, especially when the message used is the end of all life on earth; it becomes easy for evil to be an unintended outcome. The reality is that we will always need a distribution of approaches, creating a zone of greyness between the pure and angelic, and the dirty and devilish. This is too nuanced to be promoted, so it is simpler to send a single and unifying message of doom.

Extinction Rebellion, for example, presents itself as "an international movement that uses non-violent civil disobedience in an attempt to halt mass extinction and minimise the risk of social collapse". You cannot disagree with halting social collapse or unqualified mass extinction. For many years, they have been holding protests in cities, aiming to make people take notice of the damage we are doing to the environment. The actions each successive year have been more disruptive than those of the previous years. In April 2019, in their protests in London, they halted trains by gluing themselves to them. This prevented people from using one of the most environmentally sensible transport methods to get to work, driving people into more polluting methods and disrupting essential services. The cause may be important, and the message of mass extinction and social collapse are powerful rallying calls, but they would be lost if we allowed them to become more nuanced and balanced, or to be diluted by practical considerations of our livelihoods.

In the context of a group, 'good' easily becomes a marketing message rather than a virtue and creates a vying universe of us versus them.

Niebuhr's arguments are based on ideas of original sin and concupiscence. These are terms we rarely encounter today. As our world has become more interconnected and changes more rapidly, the complex moral equations needed to deal with the niceties in meanings are displaced by more mechanical economic concepts. We implicitly accept phrases like cost-benefit analysis, even if we do not know exactly what these analyses involve or how to do the calculations. We allow catch-all statements like "it isn't personal, it's business" to excuse any detrimental impacts from these calculations, and as expressed earlier, we use the economic system as the bogeyman responsible for the actions.

These arguments take the idea of choice away from the realm of our gut feeling of what is right or wrong to the world of impersonal economic measurements. We calculate, in the rational way von Mises demonstrated, the amount of money a move to the electrification of our transport system would cost and express the benefits in terms of income provided and new business profits created. We can precisely measure all this by transforming the benefits into an amount of money and comparing this amount of money versus another amount of money that represents the cost of the continued use of the internal combustion engine. We can even project the cost and benefit differences between a transition over 10 years versus a faster transition over five years.

To protect us from accusations of naivety, we include counterfactual scenarios and estimates of margins of error. This lets us tackle difficult questions of harm in a hard-hearted way. We can weigh what the loss of land should mean to a small indigenous community and compare that versus the cost of microplastics to giant sea turtles; all this while we use our economic system as a security blanket to assuage us of any guilt. We can empathise without having to be influenced by emotions.

These calculations, however, are too complex for us to do individually. They have to be delegated to governments, environmental organisations, or businesses. We have our doubts, since most such calculations, if not all such calculations, have in the past over-promised on the benefits and underestimated the costs. If we do object, our objections are easily countered by the arguments that there is as yet insufficient evidence to sustain them. Besides, we would not really know what to object to, as these calculations carry elements that we would agree on, as well as elements which we would not agree to.

We do know, however, that the places which contribute the prices and the information to the calculations are as much prone to self-interests as the groups Niebuhr described. The calculations suffer most from the issue of *garbage-in garbage-out*. If we use data that is wrong, or garbage, for the calculations, then we should expect the results to be no better than garbage. When Greenpeace calculates the cost of an oil pipeline to Alaska, it does so with an outcome in mind that it prefers. When Donald Trump's team calculates the benefits of the same, it does so equally with an outcome in mind that it prefers. Not surprisingly, the two groups, using the same method of analysis, on the same subject matter, will produce contradictory results.

So instead of a moral conundrum, we find ourselves in an economic conundrum, and instead of vested interests of moral groups, we have the vested interests of economic groups. Niebuhr's caution still applies in this economic world; rational calculations are not devoid of the tendency to fanaticism.

Niebuhr viewed the strife for perfection as necessary, even though it can never be achieved. He dispelled the idea that we can have the cake and eat it. Ideals are, necessarily, illusions, and sustainability would be one such illusion. However, it is important that we understand that it is an illusion, and equally not to let that understanding hold us back from action. In the closing of his book he writes that an ideal "is dangerous because it encourages terrible fanaticisms. It must therefore be brought under the control of reason. One can only hope that reason will not destroy it before its work is done."

This is to say that even though the efforts by environmental movements are important, they can never replace individual responsibility. Niebuhr is very clear in believing that groups help us progress. So the sustainability efforts by companies, environment and social movements, governments, and supranational institutions are all meaningful. However, they alone can never provide the solution, as they will inevitably become corrupted.

So, while we would like society to be moral so we may be permitted a little room for our own little bits of immoral excesses, the truth is society is immoral and if all is not to be lost we need to take up our moral responsibilities. It also means that while we may share the sentiments of the environmental and social justice movements, we always need to reclaim an uneasy place for virtue within ourselves, uneasy because virtue is never easy, so we can act ethically.

So how might we act?

Niebuhr developed his ideas based on the ideas of St Augustine. Back in 387 AD, St Augustine of Hippo tackled the question of good versus evil. In his book *De libero arbitrio*, or *On the Free Choice of the Will*, he presented his ideas structured as a dialogue with a student, Evodius.

Augustine was born in northern Africa, in what is today Algeria, and during his life he saw what were then unimaginable events such as the Sack of Rome by the Visigoths. The city was held hostage, and although Rome was no longer the capital of the Roman Empire, it was still the Eternal City and its spiritual centre. The idea that it could be taken over by barbarians and that all money, goods, and slaves in the city would be demanded as ransom in return for the lives of the citizens was beyond belief. He also witnessed the Vandals invade North Africa, and he was personally caught in the siege of Hippo and died there.

Prior to his Christian conversion, he reputedly enjoyed life, a lot, earning him a place as one of several patron saints of brewers. He was a sought-after intellectual and was headhunted to the position of rhetoric professor to the Imperial Court of Milan. After accepting this, his mother arranged a respectable marriage with an underaged eleven-year-old girl, for which Augustine had to give up on his lover with whom he had already had a son out of wedlock. However, as he still had a year or two to wait for the child bride to come of age, he procured another mistress. It was about one of these moments that he wrote, as a prayer, "Give me chastity and continency, only not yet."

This prayer captures his thinking on good and evil. They are not exclusive. We are neither pure good, nor pure evil, but we exist and live our lives with the tendency to both. We do not become purely either, it is an eternal struggle. Significantly, especially for us in the context of a world where resources are limited, he did not see good as something tangible in its own right to aim for, such as money is good, charity is good, or even sustainability is good, but he saw it as the result of something avoided: by turning away, by not doing.

In his fictional dialogue with Evodius, he wrote:

> Surely evil people desire to live without fear, just as good people do. But the difference is as follows. Good people pursue this by turning their love away from things that

cannot be possessed without the risk of losing them. Evil people, on the other hand, try to remove hindrances so that they may securely attach themselves to these things to be enjoyed.

In the personal context, to Augustine, the moral choice to good is to choose to turn away from that which is not ours. We are not good because we are vegan, we are good because we turn away from demanding food from the earth. 'Don't do' becomes the key to good, just as our friendly Finn, Janne, in an earlier chapter advocated. Evil, to Augustine, comes from our desire to possess things that should not be ours.

So what are these things which should not be ours? We love possessing things. Having a nice second car, even if it sits idle much of the time, gives us a sense of success, worth and freedom. The idea that we can just use it when we want, to do whatever we feel like, empowers us to think we control our lives. Being able to drive it for the school run gives us the sense we can control our time; we will not waste it by waiting for a bus. These feelings reinforce our tendency to possessions.

When we get that second car, we are possessing the resources that can be used to make other things for other people. Having the second car for myself means that in a world where resources are finite there is necessarily less metal, leather, glass, rubber, electronics, and plastic available to manufacture other things; so we cause less material to be available for others. All these things belong to no one, they should not be anyone's to possess. It may be necessary to use some of the resources for our lives, but that does not change the false nature of ownership itself; even as we use these resources we do not own these materials.

Our economic system fools us by convincing us that there will always be enough materials, so no one needs to live without them. The reality is that when we have exhausted taking resources from each other, we end up taking them from the future. Our industries mine more ores, cut more trees, grow more produce, each supported by more advanced techniques to allow a pace that is set by our tendency to possess; this is even true for 'renewable' resources. In 2020, when the Coronavirus brought our economies to an almost standstill, the Earth Overshoot Day still fell on 22 August. This date marked the point when humanity's demand for ecological resources and services exceeded what Earth could regenerate for that whole year. So, despite the lockdowns, for over four months of the year we were borrowing from the future.

The other thing we love to possess is money.

We all need money, and without it, our lives cannot function. We also have a limitless capacity to justify how much money we need and have a whole economy focused on supporting us in our rationalisations. We want security for our future and comfort for now. We need the gardener, the cleaning person, the babysitter. We want to help our children with a flat or a buy-to-let. We need that extra holiday or at least a weekend break. We deserve all of that. We worked hard for it; we were more productive, better qualified, more clever, and contributed more than others. We should treat ourselves; we owe it to our own wellbeing, to our family, and to our kids. We gave a lot away; we are charitable, we help others, we pay our taxes. But no matter how good we have been, how hard we have worked, how deserving we are, money does not grow on trees and there is only so much of it. What we take for ourselves, whether it is in our pension returns, or in our salaries, is taken from others.

Even time is something that we demand from others for ourselves. When we demand a faster response to our enquiries, for example, we are taking the time from someone. We may feel that the time is better used by serving us, but even if that is true it does not make it ours to possess.

Augustine's idea of good, in that personal context, is asking us to look to our genuine needs. We cannot be pure good, because to live we will need resources. But, as we recognise that things are not ours to possess, we will be more likely to respond to our tendency to good by turning away. He pointed out our inclination to solve problems and to remove the hindrances as evil. This is particularly contrary to our education and thinking today.

From early childhood, the lessons we learn are that to get ahead we need to solve problems. We are taught to think outside the box and are rewarded when we present ingenious solutions. If something stands in the way of us being able to do something, then finding a way around it is good. It is good no matter whether the solution is a new invention, a repurposing of an older practice, a legal loophole, or even outright cheating. We cheer each other on, in our lives and in our work, to remove hindrances. Businesses are built around the themes of offering 'solutions'. The obvious consideration of not doing something because it is being hindered is generally met with ridicule; you have to try harder. Augustine, in contrast, suggests that good people are those who are able to accept the hindrances and turn away.

Why should we not take all the money off the table if someone else will take it anyway, even if we do not? What is more to the point, when someone else takes it, we fall behind. Turning away generally leads to worse outcomes for us, we fall behind economically and risk damage to our status and our security. There is no standing still, we fall behind if we are not pushing forward. This creates the fear of missing out, and to alleviate that fear we allow room for evil: "Evil people desire to live without fear, just as good people do" (St Augustine).

Much of our developments in economic progress, technological advances, and political representations have come about to remove uncertainties in our lives. Democratic representation allows us to vote for the people whose manifestos we can study in advance, so we have assurances of their future actions. Our central banks, for all the grief we have given them in this book about their policy actions, intervene to ensure our investments are protected from catastrophic outcomes. Technological developments in every area have created increasingly personalised environments for us, so we do not have to deal with things that are not to our liking; they erode at the same time our resilience to uncertainties. All of this makes it harder for us to turn away from economic choices and to leave some money on the table.

In a personal context, therefore, we cannot look to economic choices to decide if an action is good. Good may come about from an economic choice but that is only by accident. Because economic choices do not permit us to turn away, they cannot lead us by design to good. The choice to turn away therefore has to be a moral one, that is, a choice that is not based on economic gains. It may be, as many people have advocated, that a sustainable transition will lead to greater economic growth and that we may end up with greater wealth, but those would be coincidental outcomes. A moral choice is one we make as a response to our genuine purpose for living. It is the right choice not because it leads to greater wealth or to greater certainty, nor is it the right choice because it saves our world from destruction. It is the right choice for no other reason than just that; by choosing it, it takes us a step closer to our better self.

For the moral choice to be possible, it has to be made without fear. This means that we have to deal with the fear of missing out and all of its associated emotions. In the context of Augustine's world, fear was removed by the purpose of following God's wishes in the knowledge that God will look after us. In today's context, what practices like mindfulness and personal coaching are demonstrating is a similar desire for clarity of purpose in our lives.

In Dostoyevsky's *The Brothers Karamazov*, the Grand Inquisitor lays out the foundations of a system where our physical and psychological welfares are looked after, and advocates for this system as it provides us with comfort and certainty in our lives at the expense of our spiritual welfare. This whole system is defeated, ironically, by his own recognition that "the secret of man's being is not only to live but to have something to live for". This is to say, a purpose to living so that we can look back, at the end of each day and each period and ask, "Have we lived a life well lived?" This purpose dissolves the fear of missing out.

We may still miss out from the point of view of others but we no longer measure ourselves in that way, and our comfort and certainty come from knowing that we are following a path that is true to something more than just living. The uncertainties may remain, but to live with a purpose is to accept that there are always uncertainties, whereas to live according to economic choices and the system that the Grand Inquisitor advocates for is to remove those uncertainties. For the guaranteed removal of uncertainties, however, we need continual growth and this is not possible in a world with limited resources. So if our world's resources truly are limited, then our own economic reality will tell us we will need to abandon our economic choices and prioritise ethical choices with purpose in our lives to deal with our fears.

This has implication on how we should, or rather should not, measure successes. Even if we consider sustainability as of primary importance to us, the measure of our actions is how we have lived to our purpose, and not how sustainably we are living. The targets of sustainability may change, but our purpose should still stay true. More importantly, even when the targets of sustainability are no longer viable, say we have proof that the global temperature has, irrevocably, exceeded the target of no more than 2°C above pre-industrial levels, our purpose should still provide the force to motivate us. Living with a purpose gives meaning to our living even if the world is proven to be unliveable.

Having a purpose in our lives so we can make moral choices allows us to re-engage with the economic system. It allows us to choose between accepting the benefits the economic system is offering or rejecting them in favour of a more coherent, if less convenient, life. This recovers for us the true nature of a capitalist system. The free market is only effective when the choice of not being a part of it is one of the choices offered.

The sustainability movements set sustainability as an outcome and a target to achieve, with an importance that is above the importance of living itself. It argues that unless the world is sustainable, there is no point in living because there is no point in living if it leads to our extinction. Yet things like palliative care tell us that even in the face of death there is still meaning.

Our economic system will subvert any outward goal we set into a choice for growth. So sustainability as a goal will, as we are already seeing, simply be subverted into more growth. When we live with an individual purpose, we seek to do the opposite. By being able to turn away from economic choices, we reclaim back genuine choices from the economic system to determine our own futures. They may be uncertain, but they may also be purposeful.

This is how both Niebuhr and Augustine see the path to a better self as being linked to contributing towards a better society and how the concept of good recovers meaning through our own contexts. The important meaning to individual purpose is therefore not about what we want for ourselves, it is about deriving meaning from what we do for the community.

The entire year of 2020 serves as an example in this respect. This was the year of the Coronavirus, and writing from the UK while working closely with people in Japan the contrast in the meaning of individual and community between the two countries was stark. The epidemic started in January in China, and Japan had its first case in February. The response of governments around the world was very different. Asian and Pacific countries took a strict view of the disease and instigated early action. Japan, instead of strict nationwide lockdowns, urged its citizens to be responsible for each other. Personal responsibility was placed on making sure you were not spreading the virus. The UK, in contrast, was focused on making sure, as much as possible, that normality of commerce and activities was maintained. Personal responsibility was focused on making sure you did not catch the virus.

In my daughter's primary school in the early days of the pandemic, a pupil from a Japanese family and one from a European family appeared one day with masks. The Japanese family put one on the child to make sure any germs would not spread to others. The European family did so to reduce the chance of catching an infection.

Both approaches would work equally well, in principle, if followed by everyone. Japan's thinking is if I take care not to spread it, others will not get it. For the UK, the thinking is if no one gets infected, there will not be a problem. However, there is a difference in the subsequent behaviours between caring for yourself and caring for others.

By 13 December, Japan with a population of about 126 million people had, according to its Ministry of Health's report, 2,562 Coronavirus related deaths and 177,287 cases. The United Kingdom, according to the same report, had over 64,000 deaths for a population of approximately half the size.

This difference between responsibility to self versus responsibility to others is relevant to the question of how to make ethical choices. The United Kingdom's historic and ongoing context is an economic model based on inexhaustible resources. During its history, when resources had run to their limits, the country had been very successful in colonising the rest of the world: Asia, Australia, Africa, and America. This way, resources were always made available again.

If we imagine the country's development as a road trip, under this premise of limitless resources, it could travel as fast and as far as it wished. Resources being inexhaustible meant that the road ahead would always have been there in time, with towns established, and provisions stocked. The vehicle used will always be serviced and fuel provided. In such a world, the pursuit of individual happiness is detached from any physical constraints and so may be unbounded. Someone will be there to provide for us, build the roads, set up the towns, send in the provisions, maintain our vehicles, and moreover, they will profit favourably by our trip. For them, it is a case of 'build it and they will come', and for our part, we need to show up. So the faster we can travel, the further we can go, the more others will benefit, and our happiness will lead to everyone else's happiness. In this context, moral good reflects the notion that the better it is for me, the better it will be for you.

Japan, however, has had a different context. The island country had fundamentally lacked natural resources and had frequently had to face natural catastrophes, in addition to man-made devastations like the Nagasaki and Hiroshima atomic bomb explosions. Their attempts to conquer foreign land like during the Second World War proved catastrophic. Before that, the country was closed for more than 200 years before it was forced to open under gunboat diplomacy from the Americans. Each event left a scar.

Within recent memories, the experiences of the same metaphorical road trips would have been very different. The road would have run out many times, towns would have failed to appear, provisions lost and travellers stranded with broken-down vehicles. There, it has come to be accepted that you need the support of others to survive, so in the context where resources are scarce, the better it is for you, the better it will be for me.

In the clean-up after the 2011 tsunami and earthquake that destroyed the lives of many in Japan, over $78 million in cash was found in the rubble, and characteristically, for a society that looks to support each other first, all this money was returned to the owners.

This, as a moral setting, means that the unbridled pursuit of individual happiness in a world with limited resources is damaging to everyone, including and ultimately to ourselves.

The Thomist criteria for good and evil become more relevant when we take it to the individual level, especially if we accept the world as finite and resources as limited. In such a context, the concept of good as requiring only to match one of the four conditions can no longer be accommodated, as the scarcity of resources means that we have to question more carefully whether what we do is actually necessary, not only whether it provides benefits. Simply by questioning if all four conditions are met, we become warier of actions, and it will slow us down.

Being wary of our actions and slowing them down is good. We are the product of our innate psychology and through the marketing that sustains our economics, we will always be pulled from one direction to another. We need a moral compass that we can refer to and pit our thinking against. There will be many occasions when we will have to make a choice between taking up sure-fire opportunities to make money or turning away from them with the certainty of losing out. The only way these decisions can be made consistently is by reference to a sense of purpose.

An individual purpose is an effable thing. It is hard, if not impossible even, to define, but it exists. It is wrong to confuse it with individualism; that is the pursuit of our own ideals. Individualism is an abstract concept, but we live in a physical reality that is shared by everyone and everything living on our planet. We may claim our ideas to be ours and ours only, but we do not live on land that has not been trodden on or will not be trodden on by others. This is the fallacy of Howard Roark's argument, Ayn Rand's fictional torch bearer of individualism in her book. He did not have the right to destroy, wantonly, what he created. What he created was the design of the building, and he may have had the right to eradicate the design from his own mind. The materials and resources that were used to build the building were not his to possess.

A true individual purpose has to be centred on sharing a common physical reality with the current generation as well as with future generations.

CHAPTER 12:

REIMAGINING THE FUTURE

We need to think in terms of our whole lives
to appreciate our own purpose, away from the
immediate pressures and from the influences.
But you can't actually be ethical on your own.
You need someone else so that you can be
open and, most of all, honest.

"Where do you see yourself in five years?" is one of the questions frequently asked at job interviews. I have often asked it myself, and have been asked it on a few occasions. An internet search into how best to answer the question readily provides many suggestions. They all share one thing in common: do not tell the truth.

The suggestions are to keep our true persona hidden. A glimpse of it is OK, but if we let out our true persona, then we will not get the job. When we live our lives in this way, they become compartmentalised. It is then easy for any deeper sense of purpose to be lost.

However, when we are looking to build ethical lives, imagining where we will be in five years is a useful thing to do. When we try to imagine our futures, we should imagine not only where we will be and with whom we will be, but we should also imagine how we got there. We should think through the choices we must have made along the way, such as the jobs we took and the people we befriended. We should relive the emotions and the feelings of those decisions. In other words, we need to build, as well as we can, complete pictures of those five years because they will help us to understand who we are.

When we build our ethical lives, we must build them around who we are. We cannot build them around the better persons we imagine we would like to be. Suppose that we are an unfit and overweight heavy smoker, and we imagine ourselves becoming a fit and athletic person who gets up early to help our neighbours in fitness training. If we try to build an ethical life around this fit and healthy version of us, then we will be setting ourselves up to fail. What the imagining is telling us is maybe that helping our neighbours is important. This understanding is what we need to build into our lives, and that is the life of the unfit and overweight person.

The focus of the imagining is, therefore, not to predict the future, but to understand what the things are that we rely on to guide and motivate our thoughts and actions. This will help us to uncover the things that we are taking for granted, and the kinds of people we are beneath the compartmentalisation of our various personas.

In 2015, Greece was facing bankruptcy. A new government had been elected in January of that year on an anti-austerity platform. Despite two previous bailouts, the financial situation had not improved, and the country's economy was in a tailspin with the population living in hardship. On 5 July, the people of the country were offered a referendum on a third bailout package, and the radical left government was asking them to reject it on the basis that the conditions attached were too harsh and unreasonable.

Letters from the Future is a developing technique in social sciences to help people understand the things which matter to them. The method involves imagining the future and writing a letter to ourselves from a perspective of wisdom and experience. Below is an extract from a letter that was written days ahead of the referendum in Greece. It is a letter from the future three years ahead. It was reported by Anneke Sools in the *International Journal of Social Research Methodology* in a special issue on *Narrative Sense-Making and Prospective Social Action*.

The city where I am from

3 years from now

My dear self,

I am in my childhood bedroom; it is night-time, and I am tired […]. And as it happens a lot lately, thoughts from the past, old anxieties and dilemmas flooded my mind. How did I get to this point? How did things get to this point? And the most important, where do I go from here? The referendum of 2015 seems like it was so long ago. It is 3 years ago, but in my mind it seems like it was in another life. The unrest, anxiety, fear, decision making. I was sure that I would vote NO from the very first moment. The propaganda from the channels, the people who supported the 'Yes' vote and the manner in which they did this, constantly nudged me toward the NO vote. I resisted, struggled, I would choose to take the risk rather than to stay in a horrible situation because of cowardice. I advertised the NO, I fought for it and that Sunday morning I woke up to go with the same fortitude to vote. I was never the type of person who became fanatical with political situations, but things had gone too far. […] I went to the voting centre, and decisively entered the voting booth. I had the ballot in my hand, it would not take a long time, I had told my parents to wait for me so that we can all leave together. I take the pen in my hand and I almost place it on the NO box. But I did not do it. The only thing that I remember is putting my vote in the ballot box, having voted yes. What happened? How did this happen?

As much time as will pass, I will always travel back to that moment, where everything transpired without understanding why. I remember my panic. I remember my hand trembling. I remember complicated thoughts. "You are going counter to this just to go counter", "You are not making informed decisions", "You are not thinking of those who have much more to lose", "Are you ready to take the risk, are the others ready?" [...]

It was the moment that something inside me changed. I recognized that I was not the person I believed I was. I was not a rebel. Very difficult days would transpire... and I deserved them.

I finished my studies, tried to find work, the plans for graduate training fell apart because of economic difficulties and one failure followed the other. The economic situation in the country got worse. [...] But the main reason that I have ended up here in my childhood bedroom having given up every hope and dream, was not the political situation. It was my vote, the realization of my fear. It was the moment that will always haunt me. Because we are our decisions. And I chose fear, hence it will accompany me in life. My dear self, who is reading all this, I do not impel you to vote no [...] I advise you though, to think about the person you will become [...].

Inside the chaos that exists in your brain, try to get rid of fear. Don't become a coward. Don't become me [...].

The letter reveals the personal and public emotions of the period. It imagines a future where things had not worked out and importantly reveals the author's own expectations and regrets. The final piece of advice is "to think about the person you will become".

Try now to take a pause and think about where you see yourself in five years.

When we think of our future we inevitably think in terms of achievements and successes, because we are just optimistic in that way. When we think of successes, a lot of what we imagine are the results of the expectations and beliefs we have absorbed from the things that are around us. Most of what we imagine will be dominated by recent ideas and conversations.

Now imagine a further five years, and imagine that in these five years the successes which we achieved in the first five years have gradually failed. If it were a family at the end of the first five years which we were proud of, then imagine this family slowly breaking up. If it were a success in a professional career, then imagine becoming discredited and disbarred. If it were celebrity stardom that we achieved, then imagine dropping to the D-list. If our success was in monetary wealth, then imagine slowly slipping into bankruptcy.

Now take another moment to consider this new reality.

So, when we imagine our future, we need to imagine all aspects of our lives. Our ups and downs, and our successes and failures will show us whom we rely on for support and what we rely on to motivate us, through sickness and health. Maybe we will find that neither the people nor the community we need in our imaginings exists yet in our lives, or the work and interests that will fulfil us are not what we are doing.

This exercise is doing the opposite of what the internet answers to the job interview question were suggesting. Instead of compartmentalising our lives into different personas, it is asking us to consider our whole life and explore what we rely on to sustain us regardless of what may happen. This is important because an ethical life is about the whole life.

One of the things that Richard and I did in the investment industry was to incorporate sustainability into the fund we were working for. We found for a long time we were unable to make any real headway. There was always a problem, and the root of the problem was that 'sustainability' had become synonymous with saving the world.

Our business had no pretensions of saving the world. We bought the shares of companies that we had good reasons to believe would increase in price and sold the shares of those that we had good reasons to believe would fall in price. We did this cautiously, without disrupting the companies or the financial markets, and certainly without making a noise about it. For us, profits came through meticulous and tedious labour, like hired hands who tend a garden by cutting back plants that have become overgrown and nurturing the other plants which have room to grow.

There are always some companies that are undervalued and some other companies which have become overvalued, and the buying and the selling of their respective shares help to make their pricing fairer. It was just 'work'; it produced an income for our investors and money for us to live more than comfortably. It may help the financial markets to be a little bit healthier, but we would never characterise it as saving the world.

Most of what everyone does is the same, and most of what most businesses do is also the same. We all do our little bits. Some of us, however, are vocal to claim that what they do will save the planet, and others are also vocal in declaring that if we are not saving the planet in what we do, then we are destroying it. Because these opinions are very strongly expressed, they end up defining what is and is not acceptable to be considered as sustainable practices.

Our problem was trying to fragment what we did into activities that fit with the different planet-saving initiatives. Clarifying our purpose empowered us not to be distracted in this way, but to become more aware of ourselves so that we could see if what we do is or is not consistent with a world with limited resources. It lets us appreciate how we can proceed without trying to contort ourselves into what we imagine other people are expecting.

We talked about context being important for virtue to have meaning. When the context was a world with inexhaustible resources it made sense that all activities were good; in the context of a world with resources at their limit, the concept of good as coming from not depriving others of them has more meaning. Ethical living takes that consideration of context to the individual level and applies as much to us as individuals as it would if we were a community, a business, or even a country.

Because our work was to buy and sell shares in companies that we felt were misvalued, our context had little to do with the public images of sustainability. So starting from our business purpose, which is to provide a return to our investors from the opportunities presented when companies become mispriced, sustainability means recognising that there is a natural limit to the returns we could produce. It therefore means we should accept not investing in a company that is overvalued even if it plants trees to save the world, and as a result its value may continue to increase. Planting trees may be sensible, and it may even be a way to save the planet. Investing in it may make us more profits. However, when such a company is already overvalued, more investments directed to it would simply deprive other companies of the money that they would be able to use. Our purpose is to facilitate a better distribution of capital among all the companies.

Additional investments will also likely trigger the damaging reflexive feedback cycles we have described. We may more reasonably consider selling the shares of the tree planting company to contribute to a fairer distribution of investment money. The analogy is between giving the wealthiest person in the world more money on the basis of philanthropic work, versus taking some of that wealth away from the wealthiest person to distribute to others. Our work effectively advocated for the latter.

So back to the question we started with at the beginning of the chapter, and to why the internet answers suggest that we should compartmentalise ourselves into different personas; this is because these suggestions recognise that as soon as we become aware of others looking at us, we begin to think, "What are they expecting of us?"

I went shopping in a supermarket in the Coronavirus lockdown. The country had just entered its third lockdown, and the shop was full of people. As I was waiting along an aisle, I noticed a little girl singing while she was sat in a shopping trolley. As soon as our eyes met she paused, and when she restarted, the singing was different, and she kept glancing at me to watch for my reactions.

As soon as we become aware of being observed by others, we try to match the image of what we think they are expecting from us. This is public self-awareness. When we go to buy a coffee and the barista starts by asking for our name, our public self-awareness picks up; we become more susceptible to their suggestions and we will be more inclined to purchase the options they will be offering.

Public self-awareness allows marketing to dictate what we think of as good or evil. When this dominates, our ethical life may look ideal to others as it tries to fit in with the zeitgeist of the times, but the changes and turns of fashion have no genuine meaning to us. This is like a life spent alternately switching between using paper bags and plastic bags according to whichever is reported most recently as beneficial. We will conform to the narrative of saving the world at every moment, but most likely our actions will simply contribute to producing more growth and more profits.

Back in March 2020, I received a charity campaign email in the run-up to Easter. It was from one of the organisations we dealt with and was addressed to me personally; it was sent from the mailbox of a contact I know. For this coming Easter, it stated, their company wanted our help to continue a charity Easter egg drive. The email stated that a similar drive was done the year before and was considered a huge success. My contact asked me to donate an Easter egg which would be collected and distributed to children in London. Their target was to double the number of eggs donated from the number achieved in the previous year.

At that time, Richard and I were debating how consumption comes about. I made the point that it was insidious and that most of us were not even aware of our consumption. The target of doubling the number of Easter eggs felt wrong. I was all against it. If the purpose of the campaign was to benefit children through donations, were Easter eggs the best way to do this? Might it not have made more sense to donate money to an organisation already working with children in London? To the point of our increasing consumption, if the previous year was already a huge success, as they claimed, then why was there a need to double the number of eggs?

Or, was it that doubling the number of eggs was the easiest way to double the number of clients involved? Their marketing or social responsibility departments could then claim to have doubled the good they did. However, by doubling the donation we would also double the consumption of Easter eggs. Richard called me a cynic. My sense was that there were better ways to benefit children in London, and personally, I would have been more inclined to give to the homeless person that sold the Big Issue around the corner from our office. In the end, I was nudged by the sense of public self-awareness, created by having an email sent to me personally and from someone I knew, into making a contribution. As I did so, it rationalised away the doubts that I had about my own planned chocolate excesses at Easter.

Public self-awareness not only erodes our sense of proper ethical action, but complying with it has the tendency to allow us to rationalise away further excesses. When we give to a charity, the sense we have done something good also allows us to be more relaxed ourselves about our own vices. This is the thinking behind buying carbon credits to rationalise flying, or to accept net-zero carbon plans as the way to achieve sustainability. Both these approaches are actually justifying creating emissions, and typically creating more emissions, by an action that in some future may lead to an overall reduction in atmospheric greenhouse gases. It is like buying home insurance while you burn the house.

The reality is that ethical actions come with a price. We will lose out in one way or another, but we will gain a better sense of who we are. When we think ahead and imagine our futures, a simple litmus test of whether this is genuinely an ethical life we are building or not is simply by asking whether there are costs we have to bear or not. These costs may be losses of earnings and savings; they can also likely be higher living costs, greater uncertainties, or substantial inconveniences.

Private self-awareness is the sense we have about ourselves. This is the awareness we need to develop for our purpose. It should guide us to answer where do we see ourselves in five years. Public and private self-awareness go hand in hand, however, and it is not easy to separate one from the other.

Suppose we are that unfit and overweight person we alluded to earlier, and we see advertising for electric vehicles and announcements that the sale of non-electric vehicles will be banned in 10 years' time. What should we do? Public self-awareness will lead us to respond by purchasing an electric vehicle. It does not take account of our own context as the basis of ethical action, but considers good and bad in terms of the context of the external group. Electric vehicles are good, especially for the manufacturer of electric vehicles that is paying for the advertisements. So more purchases will equal more good, and it will be good for us to do our part to purchase one.

Responding to this unfortunately takes up a lot of our time, which hinders us from being able to reflect on our own private self-awareness. We are nudged into spending our time researching electric cars and finding out which is the better make and model.

Electric cars, however, are not emission neutral. Writing in a transportation and land use news website, Conrad Zbikowski compared the carbon emission of four different models of electric cars, using data from the US Energy Department's Alternative Fuels Data Centre. The models were a 2015 Toyota Prius, a 2015 Toyota Prius Prime, a 2020 Tesla Model Y, and a 2021 Ford Mach-E. Just getting a Tesla built will cause 20 metric tonnes of carbon to be emitted, the third-highest of the four car models. This is emission before the car is even used, and it equates to the amount of emission a conventional internal combustion engine may produce after 100,000 miles of travel. If we think an electric car means no carbon emission, then we should think again.

So let us go back to that hypothetical unfit and overweight person we have assigned ourselves as and ask, what might this mean? In the reimagined future, we realise that being involved with our neighbours is important. Does an electric car make any difference to this? If we already have a conventional car, as most of us do, then switching to an electric car is unlikely to change what we do. More importantly, a better way to be involved with our neighbours is to spend more time with them, and this may mean we may want to drive less to free up some time.

It may mean we have to give up on some activity and lead us to reconsider swapping the time spent driving for more personal interactions. The result of this would also mean less carbon emission from less car use if we kept our current car, and also less air pollution from less car use. As soon as we stop using the car our carbon emission from driving stops. However, no one will see the benefits of us not using our car in this way. Public self-awareness will not reward us for doing something that is true to our own purpose.

Now think about what happens when we start to use our car less. It is inevitable that we will exercise more as a result. We will likely walk a little more, and we will carry things a little longer. These are inconveniences, and may actually be quite difficult depending on just how overweight and unfit we are. However, the economic cost of obesity was estimated by McKinsey to be over $2 trillion, which is comparable to the cost of all armed conflicts or the total healthcare costs related to tobacco use. The incentive from businesses is for greater healthcare to deal with our increasing weight issues, as these issues will generate continuous demand for services. They are good for growth, and for profits. Public self-awareness, therefore, tends to promote the right to being overweight, while hiding the environmental and economic costs associated.

So, if we are able to walk a little more, carry our shopping a little further, spend our time with our neighbours a little better, we will end up pursuing our own purpose better, and we will contribute to the sustainability issues in our own way. Of course, these benefits will not be recognised, and we will be punished with higher road taxes and charges for keeping an internal combustion engine vehicle.

The impact of responding to public self-awareness does not stop there. Because it looks bad to own the conventional car and is increasingly costly to do so, we trade it in. This means someone who does not care as much about emissions will buy it to continue its use. So the emission from the fossil fuel car continues. It does not stop there. The charging infrastructure for electric vehicles around where I live is horribly lacking. Being in the centre of London, there are charge points at every several hundred metres.

A single charge point needs to service a few hundred households, and it is clearly insufficient; we therefore need to accelerate a rapid build-out of charging infrastructure. The build-out will cause more emissions to happen and creates congestions that can go on for years. All this is advocated through public self-awareness versus, again, the alternative of having fewer cars. Public self-awareness helps us all to feel and look like we are doing the right thing, but it does not care as much as our private self-awareness about what really matters.

Private self-awareness is more likely to open the possibilities to an ethical life because it is not proposing a solution. It is not prescriptive; it does not say, "Get an electric car!" or "Send an Easter egg!" It is reflective; it asks: "Who are you?" and "Does having a car make you a better or a worse person?" These reflections take time to develop, and they challenge us to rethink our choices. It is a life-long endeavour.

Public policies too are trapped by the image of doing the right thing. Emission Analytics, an independent emissions testing organisation, highlighted friction of vehicle tyres with road surfaces as a dominant source of air pollution, especially for the very fine particles which are the most damaging to our health. The UK government's own Department for Environment has also reported on the issue. Electric cars are exempt from pollution charges even though they are much heavier and consequently create more wear and tear from friction. However, public policies do not mention the pollution associated with electric cars. Policymakers are equally influenced by public self-awareness to be seen to be taking positive actions, and so they deliver policies that allow activities to continue and encourage more growth by promoting a city full of electric cars, without tainting their clean images to conform to public expectation.

Japan has been experimenting with imagining the future in policymaking. Conventional surveys and public inquiries typically elicit strong feelings about current issues and issues which are in the public eye. These would typically focus on short-term aspects of ongoing problems, such as traffic, tourism, youth, housing, and facilities provisions. Vying camps would argue from points of view that are often based on opinions about economic developments and wealth gaps. These are all reflections of public self-image.

As no one speaks on behalf of future generations, genuine long-term perspectives are hard to achieve. Conventional approaches to decision making are inherently short-sighted because we are inherently short-sighted. We need to focus on surviving today before we can arrive at a tomorrow.

In a small-town community in Yuhaba in Japan, which has a population of 2,500, an approach called Future Design was used to complement the public consultation processes. It was part of an exercise to see how long-term welfare could be considered by including in the consultation a population of future people. These are people who are living in the town 30 years ahead of us.

At the deliberations carried out in May 2018, people who were living in the town in the year 2048 were invited. The past tense is important. They were people who were already living in the town in 2048, not people who will be living in the town in 2048. Their views were therefore based on their actual experiences of the town's various transformations in the intervening years.

A group of citizens were selected and the task assigned to them, with suitable coaching, was to be the representatives of an Imaginary

Future Generation. As part of the exercise, they were to consider themselves as residents of the same age and gender, but with different social statuses from their current status. The experiment found that the crucial turning point came when the future generation began to speak about actions as things that happened in their past. This led to them developing a retrospective perspective. Their temporal horizons then broadened away from the immediate issues, and with it, their geographical perspectives also expanded. They were more able to focus on the core needs of the community, such as landscape and environment, disaster prevention, and generation exchange. These applied across all generations. In that way, they also redefined agriculture as a heritage industry.

In a snippet of the experiment, captured in the exchange below, the first subject is speaking hypothetically as a person from the future. The first statement is about how the speaker might feel in 30 years' time, and not as someone who is now actually 30 years older, speaking from the year 2048 instead of 2018. The Secretary and the Facilitator point to the error and prompt the group to make the transition. This enables a second person, Subject 18, to comment on the value of the mountain remaining and lead others later on to express how they appreciate them.

> (Subject 23) "... If 30 years later, when I am here, if college students and townsmen are separated, I will feel a bit sad, so I hope to make warm relationship now. If you do something more and more to promote communications, it will make the town better for newcomers, and it is good for those who are originally there too."

> (Secretary) "Everybody, it is now 2048, so now is 30 years from now."

> (Facilitator) "I should have done it 30 years ago."

(Secretary) "Yeah, yeah, if I had been doing it for 30 years, it would be growing now!"

(Subject 18) "Thirty years ago, I did not build tall buildings, I did not touch it, so the mountain remains!"

The point is not to think of what we should do now to prepare for the future, which is what would happen if we think about the future from the point of view of the present. In other words, just as our reimagining is not about predicting the future but about identifying what we need to sustain our purpose, the exercise of Future Design is about identifying the core needs of the community. These are the needs that provide purpose to a community for the current and for future generations.

The group from the Imaginary Future Generation had young and old people alike. The needs that are revealed therefore reflect the differences in emotional and physical developments of people in different age groups. For our own reimagining, however, we need to include our psychological maturation as we age.

Erik Erikson, a developmental psychologist who started his career working in a Montessori school and became a major influence in the understanding of how we mature, characterised eight stages of psychological developments.

The first four of these stages take place in our infancy and early childhoods. In our teens, the question of identity dominates. Building social relations are important events for us at this stage to allow us to explore questions such as "who am I?" Our friendship groups and social settings lend shape to our sense of personal identities and determine how well we may be able to relate to others.

In our 20s to 40s, our growth is dominated by the development of enduring and meaningful relationships with our friends and families. The intimacies that develop are consequences of sharing ourselves emotionally, and emotional isolation results if we are unable to do this.

In our middle adulthood, ideas of generativity are important for healthy developments. Erikson introduced the term generativity to describe the need at this stage of development to transcend our own personal interests and instead to connect and contribute to the younger generations. In our later years, we become reflective and consider questions such as "Have we been happy?" and "What are our regrets?"

Successful transitions across these phases allow us to gain a sense of satisfaction and wisdom, even when finally we confront death. Our reimagining of the future should help us avoid ending up on our proverbial deathbeds thinking we have spent too much time at work or too much time at play.

These psychological developments can easily be lost when our lives are compartmentalised or when we are overly influenced by public self-awareness. These considerations are all about our relationship with others, whether these are our friends, partners, immediate and extended families, or simply acquaintances. When we incorporate them into our sense of purpose as central pillars, our purposes become fundamentally other-serving; in the context of a world with limited resources, they are the reasons how an ethical approach based on following our own purpose can result in sustainability.

Patek Philippe, the luxury watchmaker, has a 'new generation' ad. It is one of the most expensive brands, and its watches are highly prestigious. The catchphrase to the new ad is, "You never actually own a Patek Philippe, you merely look after it for the next generation." This may be argued as an attempt to hijack the sustainability message to fulfil our self-serving interests, but it can also be a powerful example of how other-serving action can be found even in luxury goods.

How do we know which it is?

First of all, our gut feeling will probably tell us. Trusting our gut feeling is a central tenet to behavioural ethics. This is a branch of practical ethics that has grown out of the academic areas of psychology and moral philosophy, and it is increasingly introduced into business courses as part of good business practice. James Rest, a moral psychologist who developed the field, pointed out that there are four elements to achieving ethical behaviour.

First, we need to be able to recognise if there is an ethical issue or not. This is known as moral awareness. This is where we need to be particularly careful with what public self-awareness leads us to accept as sustainable behaviour. It calls for us to look beyond what these messages may be saying, and to look in our own contexts. If we use the Patek Philippe watch as the template for our consideration, the question is not whether it is ethical to own a Patek Philippe or not, but whether it is ethical for us to own a Patek Philippe or not. This will allow the question of whether it is right to spend $50,000 or not to be asked in our specific context. Maybe our context is one where this will be engraved as a tangible legacy for our children to remember that things are precious and need to be looked after. Maybe we were paid a significant bonus and this is for us to celebrate our success. These are significantly different contexts, and moral awareness needs to recognise that they are different. Most of all, it should also not allow recognising them as different to be a justification for rationalising away our ethical purpose.

Next, James Rest points out the need for a decision. This is to make a rational case for the choice we wish to take. At this point, the gut feeling which led us to think that there may or may not be an issue needs to be examined through rational reasoning. Otherwise, our behaviour will become self-reinforcing through our emotions. This leads us to the third element. This is probably the hardest element because it requires honesty: it is to question our intentions.

We are rationalising animals. As a participant in a survey on ethical behaviour described, "It is almost a talent." We use rationalisation to justify why our actions are ethical even when they are not. Some of these arguments are very convincing, especially when they are aligned with popular and academic views against economic developments and wealth inequalities. For example, *social weighting* is a class of common arguments where we ignore whether what we do is right or wrong by highlighting someone else who is acting in a worse manner. We use the fact that some rich person is spending $50,000 on a Patek Philippe watch to excuse ourselves from a purchase of a cheaper watch which we clearly do not need. This argument extends to blaming people who use more than their fair share of resources for the demise of the planet instead of addressing our own consumption.

The *appeal to higher loyalty* is another class of common rationalisations. This is the part where we either claim we are "taking one for the team", or that we are simply operating under a higher moral authority. For the wealthy person, this may be creating a convenient case that the Patek Philippe watch is for my children *to be*. They may not be born yet, but just in case… Finally, another common rationalisation is *euphemistic labelling*. This is where we give what we do a nice-sounding label to justify what we are doing. For example, the person with the bonus buying the Patek Philippe watch may call it a reward for hard work, and so explains away any need for the action to be examined.

The only way to stay honest is to talk through the decisions and their reasons, as well as the gut feelings, with someone who can be trusted to call us out. It is not a matter of whether we are good or not, we will always want to rationalise our actions. If we therefore find that we are never called out, then we are either not honest with ourselves or maybe it is time to find a different person to talk with.

When we examine, in our own contexts, to see whether we might be rationalising, it is helpful also to consider using a veil of ignorance. This is a procedure introduced by moral philosopher John Rawls. The approach would be to decide on the action, and then consider how we would view it if our situation were different. For example, if we were the wealthy person making the purchase decision for a Patek Philippe watch, we may consider what we would think of this action if we were in the opposite position of wealth. This will help to even out the privileges of our social status and to broaden our own contexts.

James Rest's fourth and final element is of course moral action. As an individual, it is hard to feel that any step we take alone is sufficient. Taking individual actions can seem pointless when we are asked to justify what we do in terms of saving the world. The little we do will always seem pointless, especially when as the saying goes, "The Devil has the best tunes." Whatever we do from an ethical perspective as an individual will always be a tiny contribution on an economic level. However, the basis of the decision is not economics. It is also not based on macro outcomes like the future of the planet. The basis is personal and ethical.

The pressure we are putting on the planet comes from the sum of tiny contributions. When there are so many of us, the small harms made by lots of people accumulate to more than the sum of the large harms made by a few. The harm done by the many outweighs the harm done by the few. When we are one of the many, rationalisation lets us focus on our needs and ignore our harm. It is also important to recognise that in the overall context of a world with limited resources, if our moral deliberations make us slow down and reconsider what we do, we will be helping to slow the growth and the focus on profits.

Furthermore, when we choose to do what we believe is right and what our gut tells us is right, even when it carries a cost, and we are able to communicate that to others, it has the power to challenge others to do the same. This is the *power of one.*

The *Marvel Comic* series *Agents of S.H.I.E.L.D* features a group of people who work tirelessly in the background and repeatedly save the world so that others who are rich and famous can take the credit. As the series progresses, new threats appear and the actions that save the planet at one moment end up causing the next crisis. In the end, it all becomes hopeless. The group travels backwards and forwards in time to avoid and rectify the damages that are literally shattering the planet. The character Jemma Simmons is a genius biochemist in the series. She is also the sensible voice and is known for saying in the middle of all the panic and drama, "The steps you take don't need to be big, they just need to take you in the right direction."

CHAPTER 13:

EXPERIMENTATION – A WAY FORWARD

Everything we need for ethical living
is already there. It is just a matter of
experimenting with how to put it together.
Start now and start small.

In the internet archives, there is a clip from the 1970s. It is called the *New Alchemists* and is a film that was made by the National Film Board of Canada in super 8 format, complete with streaks, faded colours, and old school magnetic sounds. It looks like a film of a hippie commune playing at living off five acres of land in Cape Cod, Massachusetts.

As the film progresses, it transpires that the people involved are top scientists and agriculture experts. They also have news editors and ex-military staff helping them in their project on experimentation. Focusing on the restorative processes of nature, the New Alchemists plan to rediscover and record how to build a sustainable farm by starting small.

First, they grow a single crop. When this is established, they experiment with other things to explore what can be added to complement each other. The focus is to identify the elements which are mutually beneficial so that the combination becomes stronger and healthier. This is then continued; more crops, animals and even technologies are added to build something which grows and develops independently as a whole. This is part of a nationwide effort to get people to experiment for themselves to develop organic farming. Their results are fed into a database so that anyone interested can benefit from their knowledge and experience.

Throughout the experiment, they deliberately work to a budget. This is because we already have the plants, animals, technologies, and know-how necessary. It is only a matter of appreciating what we have and how everything can work together to achieve a self-sustaining experimental farm. The starting crop encourages earthworms to thrive; seeing this, the New Alchemists recognise the possibility of keeping fish; the pond water then provides the opportunity to farm midges as more food for the fish; chickens and rabbits are introduced; more plants are grown; technologies like windmills are introduced for both mechanical and electrical power. Progressively, but very gradually, a self-sustaining system develops.

The New Alchemists are scientists. As part of the experimentation, they meticulously document the effects as different things are changed. This all helps to provide evidence that either supports or counters the ideas that they have. This evidence then enables them to proceed with real knowledge that can be used to test different theories. They study the effectiveness of sterilised sewage and compare that against horse manure as fertilisers for different crops. They examine the influence of a dome versus a flat shape for pond coverings and test the efficacy of introducing predators to manage fish populations. They explore different methods of water filtration to keep ponds healthy. Even the efficacy of using wind energy is monitored. In other parts of the farm, they carefully record and measure 400 cabbages grown to compare the level of natural resistance different varieties have to pests. As the film progresses, they talk about growing marigolds as companion planting to repel insects and test versus growing plants that attract insect-eating birds.

The experimenters are not aiming to live self-sufficiently in a little Garden of Eden, and only a few of them actually live on the site. What they are doing is reaffirming that we can rediscover a healthy relationship with wind, waters, creatures, and soil. One of them, Dr Bill McLarney, had this to say:

> I think that one of the nice things here is that you are not detached from what's going on in the world, and yet I don't have the feeling that I am required to change the world, which I think is a pretty foolish feeling - once in a while an individual might come along who does - but I think if you can conceive of directions that the world might go and pick the one which you think is right, and get your own tiny little force behind that direction, and not be expected to... to... rush with it, and have a hell of a good time while you're doing it, that's the thing to do.

We have described how we might reimagine ourselves living an ethical life. An ethical living, however, does not come about miraculously. It emerges bit by bit as we explore elements that help us to lean towards ethical rather than economic choices. The right elements will expand our possibilities as they are integrated into our lives, helping to remove our fears of missing out, and strengthening our ability to take further ethical action. This is a slow and gradual process. We will still need to live and that will compete with our better intentions. There will be setbacks and blind alleys, and it will not be a smooth ride. This is the nature of having to deal with choices that are not economical.

The way to proceed is to start with small steps, with something that does not put too much at risk. Take for example that hypothetical unfit and overweight person we described when we were reimagining the future. We recognised in the context of that person a meaningful life included better interactions with the neighbours and also included becoming healthier. Experimentation can be used to introduce changes to our diet. The key point is that experiments can be open-ended; they do not necessarily have to be tightly defined or to conform to any image of experimentation we may have had from our school days. What matters and distinguishes experimentation from randomly trying new things is a conscious effort to reflect on the evidence to discern what works and what does not work. It is a continual process of trial and error.

Since interaction with our neighbours is important to us, as the previously described overweight and unfit person, experimentation can be used to engage them in our diet changes. We can discuss what we are trying to do, and see if they can help. We can reflect on the interaction to see if any particular approaches are more effective at producing better interactions. Maybe this comes from sharing recipes, or maybe it comes from shared meals. The point is to remember the purpose of the experimentation is to identify those things that can help us to build and sustain an ethical life.

So, if the experiments can be anything we like, and the essence is *reflection* and focus on progress through evidence, then they do not have to be about big projects. In fact, smaller ones are easier to start and have the benefit that by starting we are more likely to find ways to continue. If again we think back to the unfit and overweight person, who is now experimenting with new foods and incorporating them to improve the neighbourly interactions, experimentation in the spirit of the New Alchemists would urge us to continue further. There may other things which may be worth trying.

Keeping in mind that the basis of ethical action in a world with limited resources is the sharing of those resources, we may consider what we want to do with the electric car we finally purchased but which still sits idle much of the time. With apps like Veygo in the UK, it is possible to get insurance from a few minutes to a day at little cost to use another person's car, with their permission of course. Car sharing can become quite affordable. Sharing, however, can be quite contentious. Not having to share is why we prefer to have our own cars in the first place. Thinking of sharing as an experiment may help to avoid potential contentions. We can clarify the motivations and uses from the start and set a time limit even, and with the intent to reflect on whether this helps to strengthen our relationship with our neighbours. Maybe we find that this is also able to change our pattern of car use, and so allow us to consider sustainability options without distracting us from our purpose of living.

When we start by experimenting small, it means that we are naturally limiting our demand for resources. Even if there are many of us, each of us will be trying something different. The aggregates of our different actions will not create the same pressures as if all of us are pursuing the same solution. Some of us will look to doing less, others may find completely different alternatives, and even those who are following a similar path will have their own paces of transition. This smooths out the kind of demand surges that make for great investment stories and promote high investment returns but can easily exhaust our natural resources.

The 1995 film *Apollo 13* depicted the true events of the 1970 Apollo moon mission. After leaving the earth, 200,000 miles from home, the spacecraft suffered an on-board explosion. The crew had to rely entirely on the limited supplies they had with them to manage a safe return to earth. When we consider the question of sustainability, we are facing a similar situation. Our resources have been depleted and we have to rescue ourselves with whatever is left.

In this kind of situation, the first response is to conserve the remaining resources and not to use them unnecessarily. As the film depicts, the first action is to shut down what is not essential. The teams back on earth recognise that electric power is the principal problem. Without it, nothing is going to work and whatever the cost, preserving that last bit of power is the most urgent task. For us, we are told the capacity for greenhouse gases in our planet's atmosphere is running out. Without further capacity, a cascade of catastrophes is expected. The principal task should be to preserve the remaining capacity. In this situation, it is sensible to hold back from doing things that create avoidable emission of greenhouse gases. This will allow the remaining capacity to be used by the transition away from fossil fuels.

The car-sharing experiment that we may find interesting to try with our neighbour could help us to reduce avoidable emissions. As we share the car, it may become clear that there are journeys that we have in common which could be taken together. The motivation for sharing may be supported better with the broader picture of our impact on our environment. Just like the example of the Imaginary Future Generation in Japan, a broader perspective can bring out better the core elements which are important to our relationships.

As time goes on for the crew of Apollo 13 spacecraft, other crises appear. It is foolhardy for the crew to exhaust the remaining power on trying solutions that may not work, as each attempt saps away some of the remaining power. The teams back on earth experiment to find acceptable solutions. This way, the power in the spacecraft is not wasted. In the film, as the earth comes into sight, an intense scene is displayed with Gary Sinise, playing the role of the astronaut Thomas Mattingly, crammed in a simulator while he painstakingly and singlehandedly solves the power issue to reboot the lunar landing module to be used for re-entry to earth. In real life, Thomas Mattingly missed the flight due to the fear that he might have contracted German measles. As part of the flight team, he had intimate knowledge of the details of the lunar module and was well placed to find a solution. The moment in the film portrays the tension of a life-or-death situation that is resolved by heroic action.

Mattingly gave an interview about the film in *NASA's Oral History Project*. He mentioned that while, by and large, the film was accurate, there was one point of discrepancy. This was with regards to how the film depicted him as a hero in the simulations. He wrote:

> While they were doing that, we said, "You know, I think it's time to go home and shave and wake up." So, contrary to the movie and all of those things, we didn't solve any problems in the simulator. You don't do things that way. It was a good way of conveying the story to the public that we have to work on it, but the public could never have followed the real magnificence of having this group of people laying around doing all these things pieces at a time.

Mattingly's description is a description of how problems are actually solved, rather than the images generally presented of how they are solved. The resolution comes from "laying around doing all these things pieces at a time", and not from the super-heroic action which makes for a more exciting story.

In our world today, we need to do a lot of the 'laying around'. Our businesses are looking into how they may alter their operations, and change the materials they use. The investment industry is questioning if what they do is or is not consistent with a sustainable world. Our governments are looking at ways to overcome our economic addiction to fossil fuels. These are some of the efforts that are being made, and there are many possibilities that must be explored before we can be sure of any reliable resolution. All these efforts need to be examined carefully while keeping in mind that each attempt saps a little more of the remaining capacity for greenhouse gases.

We can do some of these experiments ourselves. If we believe too much food is being flown around the world, we can experiment with growing our own. We do not need a garden for this, experimentation means we can try and see whether if it works on our windowsills or in other places we can imagine. We know plants need light, warmth and water. Tomatoes grow readily indoors and if we achieve that, it may lead us to consider other types of vegetable which could also be grown. Success may mean homegrown strawberries for our winter which can be shared with our neighbour.

If we think there is too much air pollution, we can experiment with changing our own travelling; simply altering the schedule to avoid heavy congestion periods may have broader benefits. We may end up with a more favourable work schedule for our own lives and will have the chance, if we have children, to walk them to school before our workdays start.

Creating an exciting story, however, is more the norm, and it is the opposite of experimentation. It rarely matters if the story is true or not, its function is to capture the imagination. It encourages ideas like super-heroes solving our problems, with dramatic and grand gestures. The danger of this in a world where resources are limited is not only that these grand gestures are frequently wasteful, but also that their failures become failures of heroic proportions.

Experimentation can help to bring a degree of honesty back to the presentation of ideas. Take for example the idea of developing wind energy in the UK. Rather than pledging to turn the UK into a "Saudi Arabia of wind energy", as Prime Minister Boris Johnson claimed, an approach based on experimentation may be better for exploring the possibilities of major programmes in wind energy. Saudi Arabia has one of the world's largest oil reserves and can control the marginal price of oil through its low cost of production. It literally determines the price of global energy. The UK is ranked 78 in the world as a country by territorial area; it is unlikely to have the land or sea areas needed to generate the wind-capturing capacity that can determine the price of energy the way Saudi Arabia is able to do with its vast oil reserves. Rather than encouraging co-operation on a matter of importance, a heroic pledge in this manner instigates vying camps into vehement contests.

The Royal Society for the Protection of Birds (RSPB) has serious concerns about the pledge and raises the potential for cascading consequences if the sea bird populations are decimated. Business supporters propose the construction of nesting towers far away from their current habitats. This is similar to locating social housing far away in towns and cities where property prices are cheaper, where the motivation is to maintain profits for luxury housing rather than good social integration. These nesting tower suggestions are similar in placing profit motives ahead of scientific credibility, as they have never been tested.

An experimentation-based approach would enable a discussion of these nesting towers and enable evidence to be gathered as the project develops. It would develop from a small scale, checking the veracity of the different opinions before proceeding step by step. This allows time for any ecological disaster to be anticipated and therefore avoided.

Sometimes it takes major events to shake us into recognising that experimenting is possible. One of the realisations from the Coronavirus pandemic is that working practices can be different. Unilever, a global manufacturer of household consumables, announced in December 2020 an experiment to test a four-day working week. It is offering all 81 of its New Zealand staff a four-day week without any loss of pay. In the press release, the company acknowledged the importance to do this as an experiment. These are policies that may work for some people but not for others. The trial is carefully designed, and the company is working with consultants and academics to gather the evidence. Importantly, each person can opt in or opt out of the experiment, recognising that our individual contexts are different.

Gravity Payment is a credit processing company. Since 2015, it has had a policy of paying all its employees a minimum salary of $70,000. This, according to some reports, was triggered when the owner faced one of the people working for him, who accused him of ripping him off. Since experimenting with this policy the company has been financially successful, as well as garnering very positive media coverage. It is an example of how even in areas of compensation it is possible to experiment.

We often give in to the conventional wisdom regarding the rates of pay, especially for the highest and the lowest paid workers. These basically serve to keep wages low for the low-wage workers, and wages high for the high-wage workers. Compensation is important as a recognition of our effort, as well as a fundamental need for our living. These are separate things. They are both highly likely to be very much context-dependent, on the person, the social background, as well as the nature of the job. Sensible experimentation, especially longitudinal studies that can follow our whole lives, can provide much-needed insight into how we can change compensation to serve our purposes better and reduce our dependency on money.

Experimentation is being tried at a government level. Esther Duflo, Abhijit Banerjee and Michael Kremer shared the 2019 Nobel Prize in economics for their use of experimentation in economics and policy. Their approach is to frame the objectives of a policy as hypotheses that may be tested. The tests can then also explore the methods of implementation, and arrive at a conclusion that includes insight into how policies can be more effective.

The key to their approach is again to start small. Rather than trying to implement a policy on a large scale and then testing to see if it achieved its objectives, the researchers carry out successions of small-scale experiments adapting to the evidence as it becomes available. They were asked in their earlier days what was the point of doing things on a small scale. If the issue of poverty is so great, and if the policy would benefit people, then surely would it not make better sense to try out on a large scale? Their experience was that trying out on small scales allowed more questions to be examined, and revealed better the critical aspects of the interactions with local communities. It enabled them to adjust the final implementation so that it became more effective. It was fundamentally less wasteful.

The Nobel Prize work was carried out largely in developing countries. Where could we see experimentation at the public policy level in developed countries? Experimentation can be used in any context, the issue is to design them properly.

During the Coronavirus lockdowns, the British government requested more bicycle lanes to be created, especially in heavy traffic areas. The Royal Borough of Kensington and Chelsea in London narrowed a stretch of its high street and used the space gained for bicycle lanes. It was considered a temporary experiment and was declared as a failure after an arbitrary seven weeks. The *Guardian* newspaper questioned the decision pointing out that only 0.2% of the population in the borough objected, and that many of the online objections came from people living hundreds of miles away, even from as far afield as Nigeria and the US. They were, however, included as evidence by the borough councillors as they prepared to reopen the lanes to car traffic into the Christmas shopping period.

This is an example of a poor experiment design that allows ad-hoc selection of evidence. The borough has since put reconsideration of the cycle lanes back on the agenda, after an independent survey of borough residents showed that 56% supported it while only 30% were against it and that the statements that the lanes created unacceptable congestion were false. Transport for London, the agency responsible for implementing London's transport strategy, reported that they did not observe any significant change to the level of congestion.

The introduction of cycle lanes can be managed through a process of experimentation, which can gather evidence for potential impact on the disabled, the issue of footfall to the local shops, traffic congestion, and other issues that were raised. For it to work, we need to be honest in our use of evidence.

We do not need to be statistical geniuses to appreciate when we are being selective about the evidence we are choosing. Most of the time, we know, but we would prefer an aura of objectiveness to help us get our message across. The case of European countries stopping the use of the AstraZeneca Coronavirus vaccine is a clear example. Reports sensationalised the decisions. Storytelling techniques overemphasised the emotional element of complications caused by the vaccine and underplayed scientific evidence to the contrary. As a result, it became policy by social media.

David Issacs and Dominic Fitzgerald are staff members at the New Children's Hospital in New South Wales, Australia. They published a semi-satirical article in the *BMJ*, a medical journal, based on an ad-hoc survey of what their colleagues will do in a situation where there is no evidence on which to base a clinical decision. Titled *Seven Alternatives to Evidence Based Medicine*, the article identified seven alternative approaches. These are the alternatives we rely on instead of experimentation. They are at the same time both humorous and sobering; scary because of how accurately they describe the crazy ways in which we operate.

The first alternative is *policy by eminence*: this is essentially based on the idea that you can determine the policy if you have the gravity to be listened to. A second approach is *policy by vehemence*: this is a case where the person who is the most strident is the person to decide on a policy; Greta Thunberg falls into this category. The third approach is *policy by eloquence*: in this case, the opinion of the most persuasive and silver-tongued person becomes the policy; Boris Johnson and Donald Trump are examples of this. The fourth approach is *policy by providence*: in this case, the policy is in the hands of God, but the one who claims to know God's wishes is the one to set the policy.

The fifth approach is *policy by diffidence*: this particular situation is to have no policy, which may be no better than having a policy for the sake of having a policy. The sixth approach is *policy by nervousness*: we often see this where the policy is to reduce the possibilities of being exposed to litigation. The final approach is *policy by confidence*: the authors identified this exclusively among surgeons; as people in social media are never short of confidence, this is perhaps analogous to a policy by media where the most 'liked' narrative drives the decisions.

These approaches share a commonality; namely, they do not rely on any form of verification. They are all policies that presume prior knowledge of the outcomes. This is what makes experimentation different. Experimentation is always questioning and is therefore useful when we can admit we do not have the answers.

There is a distinction between evidence-based versus experimentation. Experimentation can look to counterfactual situations, something which existing evidence may not cover. An example is in the aftermath of the nuclear disaster in Japan in March 2011, when the country's electricity supply suffered a catastrophic loss as all nuclear power plants were shut down. This was a situation where there was no evidence of how people may respond. The Ministry of Economy, Trade and Industry joined with academics and the electricity providers from 2012 to 2013 to carry out an experiment to see how households could be encouraged to reduce energy use. A small number of households were recruited and were grouped into two groups: a moral suasion group and an economic incentive group. The members of the moral suasion group were sent messages to alert them when overall energy usage was high, and the economic incentive group were sent messages of their own costs. The experiment tested to see which had the better effect during the period of the experiment and if it had any lasting influences afterwards. It was part of an experiment to understand how to guide consumer behaviour in an effort to better shape policy.

In the EU, extensive efforts are currently in place to implement a circular economy action plan. Among these are some bold initiatives, such as a move by the French government to prohibit the destruction of unsold goods. These ideas are essentially counterfactual, that is, they are about a situation that is counter to the facts available. Unsold goods being banned from being destroyed is not something that is happening at the moment. What may happen when we try to ban it is therefore something existing evidence cannot tell us. We may find that they are sold at cheaper prices with the result that more production is made, and so rather than saving resources by eliminating waste in an absolute sense, it causes more resources to be used and ultimately wasted.

We can conjecture how different approaches might impact production, but the only real way to know is to experiment. Experimentation will also allow different opinions from the producers to the consumers to be tested. Currently, in these matters, lobbyists have huge sway in the decisions. Experimentation will balance the shape of the policymaking away from being overly influenced by lobbyists' conjectures of how things will be to gathering evidence of how things actually turn out to be. It may mean more time will be needed to decide on a final form, but that is a benefit when the final form allows for the policy to be more effective. This is Duflo *et al*'s perspective on how field experiments work.

Japan is a highly advanced society, but it has been considered as a basket case for reasons of not adhering to the western capitalist views of welfare and growth. Since the collapse of its equity market from its peak in 1989, the country has suffered a persistent recession, with companies adapting to focus on cash flow to survive. That is, earning enough money from its businesses to pay its employees sufficiently so that they can work to a high standard, and therefore generate reasonable prosperity for everyone involved. This keeps everyone with sufficient income without producing high growth.

Ageing of the population is a significant issue for the country, leaving it with a higher proportion of elderly people than any other country in the world. However, the people live longer and are healthier; a large number of elderly work as part of their retirement to make ends meet. During the height of the Global Financial Crisis, Europe and the US, and to an extent even China, were compared with Japan as heading into an era of *Japanification*, where an ageing population will cause the economies to stagnate in spite of government stimuli and central bank money printing.

The quality of life, however, in Japan has not deteriorated through this period of apparent stagnation. While by western-style measures of activities and growth the country looks like it has collapsed, the reality is that the people enjoy a very high standard of living. It is perhaps much better in many ways for having failed to succeed in growth at all cost. Even when a large number of elderly live on an income that is measured as below poverty, the standard of care they receive and their engagement with society remains high. Inflation has also genuinely stayed low.

People who have rented rather than bought their main residences have fared better, as residential property prices have not risen and renting benefitted from the property having been well looked after by the owner. The stock market may have stayed subdued, but investments have been earning a small and steady stream of income that is sufficient to support people in a world where prices do not escalate. The cost of an eat-out meal in Tokyo is not much different from a decade or more ago. Importantly, the quality of goods and services is consistently and reliably high with little variation between providers so that people can feel secure about what they will get.

In late 2017, a restaurant called *Restaurant of Mistaken Orders* opened in Japan. It specifically employed people with dementia; young people who suffered from early onset of the disease and the more normally associated elderly worked there as waiters. The name of the restaurant was chosen to make clear the situation. Orders will be mistaken. The restaurant's statistics show that a good proportion of the orders were delivered wrongly, but statistics belie the enjoyment and satisfaction shared by the clients and the staff. "It's OK if my order was wrong. It tastes so good anyway."

In our world, we face enormous pressures to save up pools of money to secure our own futures. This leads us to expect and demand high growth from our financial investments. We need the money. Our businesses resort to economies of scale on our encouragement as owners to produce them. The result is we end up in a no-win competition with each other and destroy our human and environmental diversity in the process, leaving us without any means to contribute meaningfully as we age. Our only recourse is to rely on more financial investments. We cannot break this without the fear of being left without any support.

We can, however, start by experimenting with how we might live without relying as much on financial investments. The restaurant is an example of such a step. It may not suit everyone, but it does not need to suit everyone. The restaurant does not need to be replicated to cover all people with dementia. It merely points out that we can create niches where no matter who we are, we can have meaningful lives and still contribute. It relies on us as the patrons to be willing to be open and understanding. The economics of dining becomes focused on the overall meaning more than the accuracy of individual transactions. The meal matters more than the orders.

Since the early days of the New Alchemists' experiments in organic farming, we have come to appreciate that the natural world works and is sustainable because there are niches for every organism to thrive. Each organism contributes to the whole environment making it healthier and stronger. When a field is left fallow, it is the weeds and not the crops that restore fertility to the land. In our human society, investment returns are like artificial fertilisers. They enhance our ability to improve our financial wealth but reduce the richness of our social and economic connections. High returns destroy the niches we need for us to live as who we are. The New Alchemists expressed how experimentation was necessary to rediscover the natural processes.

Japan is embracing experimentation in a big way. Its science and technology policy, *Society 5.0*, is to call for experimentation to discover how to create a human-centric society. This is because the future is fundamentally counterfactual; we do not know what it will be like. Their call to experimentation is similar to the ideas we described of using experimentation to help us build an ethical life. The launching point is again to start small.

Yuko Harayama is *Society 5.0*'s *de facto* ambassador. She introduced the initiative in a TED Talk in 2018 as a baby girl. In the talk, Harayama describes the progress in the same way as describing a child learning to walk, starting to talk, and becoming aware of the world around it. This kind of approach fundamentally accepts that progress comes from trial and error, just like the child she describes in her talk would be doing to learn about the world around her. It is not the approach that we usually see, where bureaucrats with panels of experts decide on a path and the pace of implementation. *Society 5.0* is a call to accept that we cannot predict the future, even in the short term. So, instead of believing we can alter the future with our plans, targets and benchmarks, the approach is for everybody to contribute to experimenting with the care of each other at its centre to see what may evolve.

The concept is to place society at the centre, and the path is to put aside our reliance on technology, the economy, and experts, and instead, be guided by experimentation-driven thinking focusing on people. This is not a concept to create multi-trillion dollar global companies, but to enable science and technology to help us create a society where we can achieve a life well-lived.

As an example of the scale of experimentation, Japan has developed a large-scale rain simulation centre that looks into how future rainstorms may affect the structural integrity of buildings and civil infrastructure. Climate warming will change the patterns of our rainfall, including the size and density of the raindrops; our streets may be flooded in minutes and our buildings severely damaged by the water. The only way to test is to simulate, not on a computer where we can only extrapolate from what we think we know, but physically to see what actually may happen if the raindrops are twice the size and fall twice as hard. Like the New Alchemists, the data from the physical simulations is gathered so that others may use it to help them in their planning.

Sustainability should be about improving our planet's timeless capacity for life. There is no rule book for this. We need experimentation to help us proceed. It requires us to be reflective, open, and be honest to evidence. To get good at it, we need to practise.

Q&A

Q: Planting a forest will take decades, if not hundreds of years, to recapture the carbon from the atmosphere, and currently, there is really no other way to reduce the concentration of greenhouse gases in our atmosphere. We have been fighting for centuries against poverty only to see greater wealth inequality from the social side. Are we just foolishly hoping for the best, and, if not, when will we know if we have done the right thing?

A: We work at a relationship not because our efforts will necessarily make it perfect, but because we believe in the relationship so that working at it is the right thing to do. It may never be perfect, but that does not mean we don't believe in it. Often, in fact, we work at it in the face of it being imperfect.

We work to improve the world because we believe in the world, and a genuine purpose for living is meaningful because it motivates us to keep trying.

So how do we know if what we are doing is right? We can never know for sure because the world will keep changing. So we need to be constantly reflecting on what we are doing; looking at the evidence of what is happening; be open, honest, and trust our gut feelings. We need to be constantly experimenting so we can recognise changes, mistakes and progress.

It is not about achieving the big outcome; it is about keeping up the effort.

CHAPTER 14:

ALL THE MONEY IN THE WORLD

We can invest in improving our skills or in our health; we can invest in many, many ways without it being about having a pot of money.

We can even invest so that we can have a working life in our future.

Investments need to start from having a purpose, not the other way round.

All the Money in the World is the title of a film depicting a tragic episode in the lives of the Getty family. The patriarch of the family, the original John Paul Getty, was the richest man in the world at the time depicted in the film. He made his fortune through oil and structured his wealth to avoid taxes; he could not just spend his money as you and I can, but he could use as much of it as he wished to make investments. The film takes up the story of the Rome kidnapping of his grandson in 1973, a year in which there were 16 major kidnappings in Italy; John Paul Getty, the elder, steadfastly refuses to use his money for his grandson's release. Towards the end of the film, John Paul Getty dies alone and is missed by no one. The ending reveals how having all the money in the world does not make one bit of difference if you do not have any meaning in your life.

We started this book looking at investments and we return to investments. This is not a radical call to abandon the capitalist system, but there are a number of things that deserve rethinking. These apply to all of us: individuals, the investment industry, businesses, academics and research institutions, and regulators and policymakers.

Let us start with ourselves.

A realistic estimate provided by one of our children of his eventual retirement income from his company pension is a thoroughly depressing $300 a month in today's money. This is after a projected continuous contribution for 45 years. Practically, for many of us, it means that we have to abandon the idea of a comfortable retirement. If that is the case, then starting early to save for a pension may not be the best thing to do. Having a financial buffer that can provide us with room to manoeuvre may be better. This is not to say that we should never make any pension contributions; it is to say that it may be better to view pension contributions as providing us with a bonus rather than relying on it for our living.

Having a financial buffer is very important because it will allow the room to make choices that are not determined by economics. It will give us room to experiment with different choices and time to be patient to see if they do help us. If we are living from hand to mouth and under constant financial pressures, we cannot make these choices. It also means we can choose better what we consume and how to live a life that suits us.

How much do we need? The truth is the way that wages are structured and the way that our cost of living is determined makes any financial buffer hard to build up. Saving 10% of income after tax each month gives us one month's buffer after a whole year. At this rate, we would need a decade of savings to have a buffer sufficient for one year. That is why so many of us have so little savings.

Trying to save too much from our earnings simply puts us back into economic constraints, and so experimenting will help to determine the best level for each of us. However, one thing is true, having a buffer early is better.

The most effective way to be able to save enough is to increase our earnings so that we are not living from hand to mouth. Therefore, investing in ourselves is often the most important investment to make, especially early on in our working lives.

Of course, it would be better if everyone's wages were sufficient to permit a reasonable level of savings. This would enable us to have a financial buffer that we can actually draw down on, and still have the chance that it may be replenished. It would give us room for ethical actions that can alter our economic system. It is unclear if we can ever get to such a less pressured situation, but we can certainly encourage experiments and experiment ourselves towards it. It is only possible, however, if we can halt the top end of the wage distribution from propelling higher and alter the belief that the people at the bottom of the wage distribution are lazy and must be made to scrape for their living.

There are very wide-ranging implications from this. If we think about it, to have a wage level that is sufficient to support a reasonable living means that many of the services we require need to be provided at a level of cost that is accessible by anyone. European countries have a very high standard of public services, and as a result, things like private schools are an oddity rather than a norm. The education standard of schools and universities is high and is relatively consistent across all institutions. This requires a high level of public spending to establish and maintain. If we imagine a world where income could be more equal and sufficient for us to live with a purpose, then we also need to consider what services need to be supported publicly to a sufficiently high level.

The implications for investments are clear. If we want our investments to succeed by siphoning off the profits into our portfolios, then there will not be the income to governments to provide the public services. However, simply wanting something does not make it happen. The nature of governance in the investment industry and in businesses is a relic of a time when businesses were privately owned, and governance was about the founder having and maintaining control. We have now become the owners, but the management teams have taken over the control. Governance is largely reduced to voting on motions proposed by the management teams.

There have been exceptions. Small shareholders generally do not get involved with how a company is being run. However, the community of the Sisters of St Francis in Philadelphia is a counterexample. They have consistently been in the media for their actions, as owners, to influence how major companies conduct themselves. These companies included names like GE, AT&T, Toys 'R' Us, Coca-Cola, Bank of America, and Goldman Sachs. The nuns have advocated on a range of social and environmental issues. Their pension portfolio was established in 1974, and after six years of informal action, they established a Committee for Responsible Investment. Last year, they engaged with the Security and Exchange Commission (SEC), the financial markets regulator in the US, to challenge regulatory changes that would make it harder for small shareholders to propose motions. Their actions have generated more governance awareness but have also created hostility. T.J. Rodgers, for example, in his role at the time as CEO of Cypress Semiconductors, viciously attacked their proposals for more corporate responsibility. It is not often that nuns are publicly vilified by a business leader as being immoral.

The cop-out from business and the investment industry is always going to be that there are far too many small shareholders. In other words, there are too many of us. That was the reason behind the

SEC's move last year to make it harder for small shareholders to propose motions. The trend is to consider our representation under a general umbrella of an anonymous 'stakeholder', and for the investment industry to speak wholesale on its behalf. The conflict of interest this creates, however, is clear.

If we go back to the issue of paying taxes and funding our public finances, the investment managers and the people in the companies' management teams all benefit from the company paying less tax. This will improve the companies' share prices; their reward incentives are aligned with this. For us, we lose our schools, roads, hospitals, and parks. For the anonymous stakeholder, the issues tend to be about broader things like child labour, modern slavery, and climate change. These have obvious importance. However, an international company can address these issues without contributing to the public services in the countries we live in. We simply do not have the governance representation that can allow issues affecting our everyday lives to be considered.

It is not only just a matter of public services. The future of our jobs is at stake. The efficiencies from automation and machine intelligence that produce higher investment returns are enabling disruptive businesses to take over the small and medium-sized businesses that provide most of our jobs. Online accountants and online lawyers are competing against high street accountants and high street lawyers. Smaller retail shops have already lost out to online retailers, and driverless taxis are now available in China's larger cities. As owners of these companies, we should be able to choose between jobs for ourselves and profits for ourselves. This requires a different approach to governance, one that eschews a more democratic representation of our purposes. In the end, the purpose of all investments and all businesses is not to generate financial returns but to serve us as people to fulfil our purpose for living.

For those of us who are closer to retirement, our need is to access income even as we age. Continuing paid work is going to be increasingly common in lieu of retirement. This will help to alleviate our need for higher investment returns and is at the same time driven by the failure to achieve sufficiently high investment returns. Work is important for our sense of worth and for our social interactions; if we can continue it we may reduce our social care needs. These are aspects of governance that we as owners should put on the table of our businesses.

Next, let us look at the investment industry.

The investment industry and all the associated businesses have a fundamental conflict of interest. They are rewarded on the basis of the amount of money they manage. When the fees are determined by the asset size, the incentive is to push for growth. When we have $10,000 invested, a fee of 1% equates to $100 a year to the investment industry. If our investments achieve a growth of 3% a year for two years, then at the end of the two years our fees will have increased to $104 a year. If our investments instead achieve 20% each year for the same period of two years, then at the end of these higher return years the fees to the industry will be $140 a year.

This is a business that can increase the amount of money it earns if the returns are higher while advertising the fees as unchanged. In addition, each time we add a contribution to our savings, the total amount invested is increased and provides the industry with more income. With these incentives, it is easy to end up with too much money invested and chasing too high a level of return for what our planet can sustain. This leads to everything becoming financialised.

As many of our larger investment management firms are public companies, it again comes back to a question of governance. It is not an issue the industry would likely address, as the answer may require it to shrink. Ultimately, it should be our choice as owners to decide.

Another issue for the investment industry to rethink is its own ethical purpose. The industry can never paint itself as good; it is one that permits both good and evil to be carried out. It funds the ammunition companies that produce the bullets that are used by the person who kills children in a school shooting. It also provides the investments to bring about the companies that make the IV bags that are used by the paramedics as they work to save the children who are injured in the same shooting. It is a necessary industry, but necessity does not equate either to good or to evil. It must therefore be honest in admitting this, and be ethical in examining when it is right to chase returns and when it should forgo returns. The aggregate impact from the pursuit of returns is often responsible for significant damages to our planet and society, and the industry has to address and answer this.

A further issue that is related to the last point is the drive to passive investments. The transition to passive investing is highly beneficial to the industry in its current form, as the process creates a significant performance momentum. However, this is a feedback process that ignores any capacity constraints and is actually hugely damaging in many ways. As additional investments accumulate, more resources are needed to provide the same investment returns as before. This demand is blind to whether it is right to requisition further land, mines, and other resources for this purpose.

All these issues require a different communication approach from the marketing stance that is used currently. An objective reporting and a reflective stance would be better. It should be one that opens the industry to potential reparations for damages. The industry cannot mature and become ethical if it always benefits and never has to face the consequences of its actions. All this opens up the question of representation: is it acting for itself, or is it acting on our behalf?

My father's experience in his cancer treatment is an interesting example of what such a representation may look like. In his treatment, he was surprised at the time the doctors spent to get his input into his care, emphasising the dangers as much as the potential benefits of the proposed treatments. He grew up in a time when doctors called the shots. It was through decades of development in the medical profession that doctors accepted they were not masters of the patients, but their servants.

The investment industry would say that there are too many clients for this kind of interaction, too difficult to implement, and the costs will be too high. However, while this may ring true, it is also a way to rationalise away their responsibility. The issue is whether it is willing to experiment to find a way, or whether it continues to rely on rationalisations to avoid actions that may be financially costly to itself.

For companies, the central issue is governance.

When we invest in a collective investment scheme, we should not be relinquishing our right to determine how the companies that are purchased on our behalf should conduct their business, nor our responsibility for what is done. When, for example, Rio Tinto is lambasted for destroying ancient Aboriginal caves, we should feel shame ourselves for our part as the owners. We live in a culture where social media demands resignation on every failure, but it is not honest to blame the management teams when we have failed to express our need for governance sufficiently. Small shareholder action is often not welcomed by companies, and this leaves the ownership control exposed to activist shareholders who often take over a company to cut costs and to bring in different operational methods to increase profits. These actions often impact us adversely in our broader environment even if they increase the monetary value of the company. By giving up our claim to governance, we are washing our hands of our duty.

Another issue for businesses is the actual structure of share ownership. The founders of a business are able to ride on the wave of support long after the contributions are no longer from the founder but from other people. Multi-billionaires are created by a reward structure that biases against later contributors. The early entrants in the business stand to gain dynastic wealth; this creates an incentive for people to want to work in startups, and for startups to want to be particularly aggressive in pushing for growth. It encourages businesses to sell an idea rather than to generate profits that can be used as income for the investors.

These businesses have to look to increasingly massive scales to attract the investor. For example, the online fitness company Peloton has 3 million subscribers, but it is valued on the basis of a possible 100 million subscribers. Other startup businesses, such as Starlink, rely on the same model of relying on a future vast expansion to justify high valuations. Starlink is a satellite company aiming to provide high-speed mobile internet using a network of tens of thousands of low orbit satellites. It is reported to have potential for 360 million-plus subscribers to enable an estimate of $175 billion for its value.

All this makes businesses look to future promises rather than to deliver actual profits, and creates greater and greater demands on resources to support these claims rather than fulfilling current demands. It is like the difference between the mass manufacturing model that looks to use resources without limit rather than the purpose-driven production models which look to produce an income by meeting current demands.

We next turn to academics and research institutions.

As highlighted earlier, the fundamental issue is that we are the shareholder and not simply some anonymous stakeholder. We provide the money that is used to buy the shares and these come with governance rights. Therefore, we should have more say than the management teams, who are our employees.

Successful business managers, however, have a tendency to credit successes to their individual skills. It is like the age of football managers before statistics started to influence teams selection. Then, it was all down to the manager. Some managers undoubtedly had an innate statistical ability which helped them to make better selections. That does not alter the fact that a scientific approach to deciding which player to buy and sell, and which player to play in different games is possible. These approaches may not have the flair and the passion that accompanies a manager with strong instincts, but they do work and often can point out when managers are claiming credit that is not theirs.

In business, there are good managers, but this does not alter the possibility that there can be more scientific approaches to determining what are better practices to put together. Only when we have this is it possible for governance to operate properly. How damaging is it to a business if it paid tax on the revenues it generated in the countries where they were generated? With better information on how businesses work, we can better examine such questions. Is there some other operational approach that could be considered? Similarly, we could also examine questions such as, "Is it necessary for the management teams to be compensated the way they are?"

Businesses and academics should have a natural incentive to promote research and open access to the data on these issues. The investment industry should also be naturally interested. When is it better to invest in something like Amazon or Tesla, versus companies such as Walmart or Volkswagen? What is the real difference between them? The former companies are clearly much higher valued, but they also make almost no profit and do not contribute to our public infrastructure as they pay virtually no tax. Tesla's revenues are substantially smaller than Volkswagen's and employ far fewer people.

How can we understand which businesses are actually helping to reshape our society into the shape we want, rather than promising to do so? How can we have an open database that can allow these considerations to be better examined? In the end, the job of the investment manager is to decide on a rational basis the potential value of a company. Countless analysts already try to do this, each on their own, creating their own spreadsheets and databases. It is surely more beneficial for this information to be public, as the New Alchemists did with the knowledge they gained, so that it can be used by others.

Vested interests would argue that this information is proprietary and, for commercial reasons, it should not be available openly. It would be interesting to compare this claim against the existence of open databases in scientific and medical areas. In the medical field, *PubMed* and *ClinicalTrials.gov* exist to act as such databases. arXiv. org exists as an open archive for research in the sciences. Wikipedia is also a demonstration that a publicly contributed resource can become invaluable.

Governance is a fundamental issue, and to govern well, we need to be educated. Whatever the model for the governance structure, if we govern in ignorance, then we cannot expect good outcomes.

Finally, we consider regulators and policymakers.

Their role in investments is very important. They are generally seen as the agents for controlling the system. This is largely an illusion.

They have the ability to encourage the worst of the damaging feedback cycles, and the power to prevent them from happening. Policymakers still operate under the presumption that the world's resource is infinite in that they do not distinguish between productive and damaging growth. In this way, they promote indiscriminate growth.

Milton Friedman, the modern guru of monetary policy, convinced the world that the social purpose of business is profit. In his book *Capitalism and Freedom* he stated, in the section on *Social Responsibility of Business and Labor:*

> The view has been gaining widespread acceptance that corporate officials and labor leaders have a "social responsibility" that goes beyond serving the interest of their stockholders or their members. This view shows a fundamental misconception of the character and nature of a free economy. In such an economy, there is one and only one social responsibility of business to use its resources and engage in activities designed to increase its profits...

When policymakers join forces to rationalise self-interests, it makes our attempts at ethical action all the more difficult. For most of the past decade, the major central banks have provided tens of trillions of dollars to support the economies of major developed countries; this money has not made people feel more secure. Exactly like in the California Gold Rush, when more money than imaginable was freely being dug out of the ground, people just behaved worse. Individual interests got the best of everyone, the money simply drove up prices, and the ones who became wealthy did so by hoarding, making necessary goods scarce until they became unaffordable. People starved even as there was more money in circulation than ever before. The ready availability of it became a justification for more selfish behaviour. The more that money was readily available, the more those who had it dismissed those who did not, considering them as either unenterprising or underserving, or simply claiming that it was their own fault.

The Grand Inquisitor in *The Brothers Karamazov* used Christ's three temptations to lay out the purpose of a policymaker. These temptations are food and sustenance for our daily comforts, power to rule and control, and vanity to flatter our sense of worth. By providing these, the Grand Inquisitor claims, we would be sated and our lives would proceed without risk and violence, even if they are purposeless.

Regulators have a desire to support us in the same way, to provide us with the means for our lives to continue without uncertainty and distress. However, this is not possible in a world where resources are finite, as our desires and want will exhaust all of that which is available. Regulators' principal purpose instead needs to be to encourage ethical action to place the welfare of others first so that we may ourselves be served. Since money provides the means to chase relentlessly each of the three temptations, regulators can avoid putting temptations in our way by preventing the excess of money to dominate.

Regulators aim to provide a level playing field, so that the dreams of individualism where each man may pursue his own happiness with others being treated as equal are possible. However, again, the problem with a world with limited resources is that the level playing field is our planet. The planet needs to be considered as an active player. It is like a football game in the rain; the referee ensures it is fair game by checking neither team has any particular advantage, but the pitch is destroyed as the players vie for their team's dominance. We have no groundsman to call off the game.

For us, when regulators treat the planet as a playing field, ensuring fairness between the players only serves to destroy the pitch. The pitch cannot be made to become a player as the players are, but the players can be made aware of the pitch's value through their own choices, and if we genuinely care enough we may consider conceding and accept a lower place in the league so that we may play again. Encouragement of ethical action may do this better than stimulus actions that place temptations in our way, but this is only possible if the stimuli do not make the stakes so high that conceding and falling behind threatens our own survival.

Finally, humans have managed to produce and innovate through extreme situations and undoubtedly will do so again. We have tremendous capacity and resilience to develop innovations in the face of adversities, and it is a matter of trust in the purpose and ability of all people that we will continue to do so.

In the end, we do need to consider a life without our pension investments. This does not mean that we should not invest, but it does prompt us to rethink how we support each other as we age, and investments need to arise from that context.

We have always been aware that we create real harm as we grow. This recent reawakening of concerns is not new. During the industrial revolution, the mass adoption of coal led to incidences of unparalleled atmospheric pollution, and the move to an industrial society started the disintegration of rural life. The year 1970 witnessed the first Earth Day, giving voice to the public fears at the time about the state of the planet. Walter Cronkite's broadcast of the event captured the gravity of the mood with the message "Act, or die."

In 1972, the Club of Rome, an international body created as a collaboration at the highest level of government to address the many crises facing humanity and the planet at that time, published its report: *Limit to Growth*. This clearly pointed out the unsustainability of our consumption and growth paths. There was even an 'Anti-Fair' boycott of a 'Teenagers' Fair' in Sweden in 1968, mentioned in Victor Papanek's thought-provoking book *Design for the Real World*, as a rebellion against the systematic plan to entice them to over-consume clothes, cars, and status junk.

It is ultimately down to us to behave ethically. Money helps, but even with all the money in the world, we cannot depend on it to be the solution it promises if we lack purpose and ethics in our actions.

CHAPTER 15:

HAPPILY EVER AFTER

Individual actions are powerful and important. By being examples for each other, our actions shape how our world will become. We lead policymakers and businesses, and when we accept that there are sacrifices and live with a purpose, they will understand their roles and serve us. We may never know the outcome, but don't make it about the outcome, it's all about the trying.

A recent paper on 21st century forest carbon fluxes shows that the Amazonian rainforest in Brazil is now a net carbon emitter. The lungs of the planet have finally taken up smoking.

Sustainability efforts are everywhere. Governments are trying to lead the dialogue; businesses of all colours and persuasions have sustainability in their mission statements. People are involved in activist movements to force others to change what they do, if not by persuasion, then by force.

A lot of these efforts are important and we do need them. The transition from fossil fuel to renewable energy has been in the discussion from as far back as when I was at secondary school, and that was a long time ago! We read about the tidal energy plans for the Bristol channel in the UK, and about the ambitions to create solar energy farms in the deserts around the equatorial countries. In the intervening years, nuclear and hydroelectric power has been developed to provide much of the domestic energy for Scandinavian countries. Our use of fossil fuel energy has not abated though. Norway, with 80% of its power supplied by renewable sources, has still experienced a pretty much continuous increase in its oil consumption.

In the midst of the new problems, older problems still persist to haunt us. The ozone hole, though much smaller than what it might be, is still three times the size of the continental US; acid rain, though less frequent than at its peak, is still present. Our efforts matter without them things would be much worse, and things will be much worse if we do not continue with them, but they have rarely truly resolved the issues.

For all the calls on sustainability, a policy of forcing others to change is unlikely to succeed. We are too wary of the costs to ourselves if we are to give up on the temptations our economies offer us. We like the certainty of comfort and sustenance; we want to have the power to control and to rule; we live for the recognition of our good works and good characters. All these are promised to us by our economies, and to fulfil them, we contribute our fair share to promote the drive for growth and profit.

All this encourages us to put ourselves first. It dilutes ancient understandings about the nature of good and evil and replaces them with economic transactions. As long as there are new resources to be had and new technologies to expand our planet's capacity, this will work. They help us to replace the need for purpose.

Then again, maybe life is not just about living, but maybe living really is about having a purpose for living. In a world with limited resources, we are all linked by scarcity. There will not be sufficient resources for us if we look to ourselves first. It is a cycle of hoarding that can only end badly for everyone. Any purpose has to look towards being other-serving, as resources have to be shared. In this world, good does not come from achieving a result, but from holding back from fulfilling our desires. In this world, sustainability is something that happens because we look to change ourselves to look after each other.

The *Wizard of Oz* tells a story of how a young farm girl from Kansas is carried away by a tornado, and in her search to find her way back home she exposes the folly of following a road of gold and believing in magic to control the future. The wizard is the first central banker, frantically moving the levels of the economic system to try and fulfil the promises of comfort and security. Along the way, she discovers that all she needs to face uncertainty is courage, heart and mind. Her path is impeded by many obstacles, including the Wicked Witch of the West.

In the ABC TV series *Once Upon a Time*, the Wicked Witch of the West infiltrates a cursed town in Maine. The characters are all from Disney's fairy tales. There are good characters such as Snow White and bad characters such as her wicked stepmother, the Evil Queen. They are thrown together into the small town by an evil curse that takes away the chance of ever finding a happy ending. Each time they defeat evil, a new curse is cast. The Wicked Witch of the West arrives just in time to cast her curse.

After repeated failures, the characters, good and bad, finally appreciate that it is not about happy endings. With the courage to make ethical choices, a heart to care for each other, and a mind to guide them, they can always hope for happy beginnings.

Whether sustainability is achievable or not is irrelevant. What matters is with what purpose do we start.

About the Authors

Dr David Ko

Dr David Ko started in investment management in 1994 with LTCM as one of the first people to be employed by the hedge fund. Before this, he was a university lecturer in physics at Oxford University. Its meteoric rise, with the Dream Team of market wizards, central bankers, and Nobel academics, triggered other market participants to jump on the bandwagon of its strategies until the collective demise came to within a hair's breadth of global financial Armageddon. It was his first and constant reminder that investing for profit has devastating consequences.

After a successful career in investment management, he sidestepped the Global Financial Crisis by taking a sabbatical running Science Investigators to deliver hands-on workshops to schools. He later returned to investment management and worked since 2017 with Richard looking at sustainable investing. This led them to recognise that the problem is we simply have too much money invested for the planet to provide the returns without destroying it.

About the Authors

Richard Busellato

Richard Busellato grew up in Sweden. He worked in Stockholm in 1990 and later in Brussels for some of the world's oldest corporations before moving to London 25 years ago. He has been involved in investing throughout this time, successfully navigating some of the most volatile periods in the financial markets. Famously, he remembers his first lesson in risk management – imagine the worst that can happen, and double it. To this day, this remains a defining consideration to how to see the world and what is happening in it.

He worked in many of the premier hedge funds and financial institutions, taking senior roles with responsibilities over large investment decisions. He joined with David and researched not just the financial but also the driving social and ethical aspects of sustainability. This led them to the idea of Rethinking Choices – a holistic examination of how we can genuinely contribute to the planet's timeless capacity for life.

NOTES

NOTES

NOTES